HIV Infection and Children in Need

Edited by Daphne Batty

British
Agencies
for **A**doption
and **F**ostering

Published by
British Agencies for Adoption & Fostering
(BAAF)
11 Southwark Street
London SE1 1RQ

© BAAF 1993

**British Library Cataloguing in
Publication Data**
HIV Infection and Children in Need
    I. Batty, Daphne
    362.7

    ISBN 1-873868-08-1

Designed by Andrew Haig Associates
Cover photo graphic by Jeni Mckenzie
Typeset, printed and bound by Russell Press (TU)
in Great Britain

Contents

Foreword

John O Forfar

Professor Emeritus of Child Life and Health, University of Edinburgh, and formerly President of the British Paediatric Association, and Chair of the Medical Group of British Agencies for Adoption & Fostering.

Throughout history pandemics of disease have periodically swept the world. AIDS following HIV infection is the modern pandemic. In medical terms it is a disease likely to cut off adults in the prime of life after a series of debilitating illnesses and years of doubt and apprehension about the future; it puts the infants of infected mothers at great risk of early death or lives burdened with anxious uncertainty; it hazards the sexual partners of sufferers. But the significance of AIDS extends far beyond the boundaries of medicine. HIV infection is a critical environmental issue with a wide range of social implications for the adults who acquire it, the babies who inherit it and the families it can devastate. It requires skilled informed counselling, it raises legal questions, it can cause ethnic and religious problems.

In this grim scenario, alternative care for affected children has an important role to play but one requiring constant redefinition in the context of a disease so recently recognised and variable in course that much remains to be learned about its nature, management and social effects. Children infected by or at risk from HIV, or orphaned by the premature death of parents from AIDS, have very special needs. BAAF recognised this with the publication in 1987 of *Implications of AIDS for Children in Care* and has recognised the need for continued updating of knowledge, understanding and practice with the present volume. This volume renders a signal service in providing an important source of guidance for the wide range of professionals who deal with AIDS not just in the field of adoption and fostering but in all disciplines which deal with 'HIV infection and children in need'.

1

1 Introduction

Dr Marion Miles

Dr Marion Miles, Chairperson of the BAAF Medical Group, is Consultant Community Paediatrician at the Medical Centre, Parkside Health Trust. She is medical adviser to two inner London boroughs and also to a voluntary adoption agency.

Implications of AIDS for Children in Care was published by BAAF in 1987 and it addressed many of the issues which arise around the placement in substitute families of children thought to be at risk of HIV infection. During the subsequent five years a greater understanding of the condition has been achieved so it is now timely to consider recent developments in relation to these children in a new publication.

As the spread of HIV infection into the heterosexual population progresses, the emphasis in the process of identification will necessarily shift. In the future, we shall be moving away from only considering those groups currently described as 'at risk' and towards considering all groups in the population.

In the meantime, while some children appear to be at greater risk than others, the nature of the different groups varies throughout the country. Consequently, agencies need to have both a broad-based understanding of the problems as well as more focused information about the characteristics of the families with whom they work locally. This collection addresses the issues that must be considered.

Transmission and prevalence

In Chapter 2, Dr Marie-Louise Newell and Professor Catherine Peckham discuss the transmission of the virus, the different sources of infection, and very importantly, they highlight the lack of evidence of casual transmission. The prevalence of infection with particular reference to the situation in the UK is reported together with the development of surveillance systems designed to monitor the progress and distribution of the problem.

Diagnosis and prognosis

The difficulties surrounding early diagnosis in infants are described in Chapters 2 and 3. Dr Jacqueline Mok details the wide clinical spectrum of HIV infection in children drawing on her experience in Edinburgh. Attention is drawn to the bimodal distribution in the severity of the clinical picture which has emerged, earlier emphasis having concentrated on the more severely ill children. It is important and relevant in the context of this book to note that one third of babies proved to be infected are severely ill and die during infancy while two thirds survive. To date it is impossible to make accurate predictions about their progress and ultimate survival. This, of course, presents problems when planning placements and identifying resources and can lead to frustration on the part of families and workers who may, unrealistically, expect more precise information from health advisers.

It is also important to note the differences between the clinical pictures seen in children and adults. Most adults with HIV infection remain asymptomatic for many years. Indeed the presence of infection in an adult may be revealed following illness in a child or partner at a point in time when the subject is well. Symptoms, when they do develop, are variable and may occur episodically with a good response to supportive treatment, thus providing an opportunity for parents to care adequately for their children for different periods of time. This variability means that respite and other supportive care should be used flexibly and with imagination. Infections which complicate HIV infection are different in the different age groups, being more frequently bacterial in nature in children and therefore requiring different treatment regimes.

Testing

Over the past few years the advantages of prophylactic treatment during the asymptomatic stage of HIV infection have been demonstrated. Thus a case can be made for greater emphasis on early identification in order to consider therapeutic options. The ethical issues surrounding testing are explored in Chapters 2–5, but at present, the case for widespread testing prior to adoption or fostering has not been made and it remains essential to consider each situation separately.

The legal aspect

The legal implications surrounding the placement of children at risk of HIV infection are discussed in Chapter 4 by Simmy Viinikka. Issues around consent are particularly relevant when testing for HIV infection and the changes in the law consequent upon the Children Act 1989 must be considered. Quite often there is confusion about confidentiality and this subject is usefully discussed within the medical and local authority context.

Social implications and developments

The social implications of HIV infection cover a wide area, different aspects of which are addressed in Chapters 6 and 7 by Carol Lindsay Smith and Joan Fratter who describe the Positive Options Scheme whereby parents infected with HIV can make plans for the future care of their children. Many of the parents thus supported to date have experienced other problems including poverty and inadequate housing. It is to be hoped that provision for these families will be facilitated by implementation of the Children Act since the children involved are certainly in need. At the same time a challenge is offered to health purchasers to collaborate with other agencies to develop flexible and reactive care programmes.

The black perspective

Hong Tan in Chapter 8 reminds us that the ethnic, cultural and religious needs of all children should be addressed as required by the Children Act. The development of appropriate services for children and families with HIV infection which also meet these needs must be supported.

The prevalence of worldwide HIV infection due to heterosexual transmission is at present higher among the black communities worldwide than the white population. However, there is a danger of assuming that a higher prevalence indicates the source of infection and this aspect is discussed in detail. Care must be taken to avoid distortion by racial prejudice of the early theories that Africa was the source of HIV infection and consequent conclusions about the transmission process. There is also a tendency to group all black communities together as a convenience when identifying resources and considering planning options. This must be avoided if appropriate specialist services are to be developed. However, examples of good practice do exist and they give cause for hope for the future.

Bereavement

Coping with bereavement is always a daunting task and especially so when children are concerned. Juliet Swindells describes in Chapter 9 the work of the Haemophilia Centre in Thanet where considerable experience has been gained working with children who are infected with HIV and their families. The importance of maintaining an open and honest approach tempered with sensitivity is demonstrated; facilitation rather than the imposition of decision-making would appear to be the way forward.

The Scottish experience

Scotland is able to provide specific experience and valuable advice about HIV infection although the situation there is different from the rest of the UK since in Scotland, 51 per cent of HIV positive reports are associated with intravenous drug misuse. The problems in Edinburgh, where 60 per cent of cases occur, involve heterosexual transmission in addition to vertical transmission from mother to child. Dr Jacqueline Mok describes the work of the Paediatric Counselling and Screening Clinic in dealing with this.

Services in Lothian have also been developed to meet the needs of families with different permutations of illness and well being which exist between parent(s) and children. There is now a wealth of experience which Gerry O'Hara draws from in Chapter 5 in which he describes the services and emphasises the need to maintain a flexible system. He also explores their selective approach to the screening of children with HIV infection who are being placed for adoption.

In all cases the co-operation of parents is sought and their wishes about testing are respected unless the child is ill. The Lothian experience demonstrates very clearly the need for all involved to understand and respect each others' roles and to develop a holistic approach to the problem.

Providing care

A description of different aspects of care is given by Sarah Ryan in Chapter 10 in which she recounts the experiences of two adoptive mothers of children with HIV infection. One example provides a truly historical account since it concerns the first child diagnosed in Scotland to have HIV infection. Despite scanty information available in those early days of 1985, the child was accepted into the family and adopted. The second example is quite different since the family offered itself to care for an HIV infected child. The uncertainties about illness and prognosis are considerable, as is the distress caused by regular hospital attendance. The differences in approach to the disclosure of the child's HIV status are described together with the problems which can arise following disclosure. The burden of care is graphically recounted. One family has faced bereavement, the other awaits it. There are conclusions to be drawn from these family histories which emphasise the issues of the stress of uncertainty on the family, hospital attendance, the need to observe good hygenic procedures and the skills and sensitivity needed to be able to share painful information with the child. There are happy times and sad times and the support has to be flexible to meet these circumstances.

Putting theory and good intention into practice can be difficult, and in Chapter 11, Sue Wates describes, with compassion, her experiences of sharing her home with people infected with HIV. They exhibit many emotions with guilt very much to the fore but the ignorance and rejection shown by uninfected contacts demonstrate the need for continuing health education for society in general. The case for the development of support networks for carers as well as HIV infected people is well made.

Finally, Daphne Batty concludes the collection with a brief summary of current developments and, on the basis of the issues raised by the contributors, sets out an agenda for all agencies responsible for working with children and their families. Workers in the field of HIV are constantly meeting new challenges and the three essential elements in working with HIV children and families are knowledge, initiative and flexibility.

The World Health Organisation estimates that there are one million children with HIV infection in the world at the present time. Mercifully, against this background, the number of children with HIV infection or AIDS in the UK remains relatively small. Nevertheless, the issues facing agencies are complex and challenging including planning for non-infected children who are nonetheless affected by AIDS. Although all the questions which can be raised are not answered, this book will serve as an invaluable record of current work and new initiatives.

2 Transmission of HIV Infection

Dr Marie-Louise Newell and
Professor Catherine Peckham

Dr Marie-Louise Newell and Professor Catherine Peckham write from the co-ordinating centre of the European Collaborative Study of children born to HIV positive mothers in 20 European Centres. This study is based in the Department of Paediatric Epidemiology at the Institute of Child Health, London.

Human Immunodeficiency Virus (HIV) is the virus that causes Acquired Immune Deficiency Syndrome (AIDS). Infection can be acquired through sexual intercourse with an infected person; transfusion of infected blood and blood products; sharing of contaminated drug injecting equipment; semen donation, tissue and organ transplants; and from an infected mother to her child during pregnancy or in the perinatal period. Although HIV has been found in saliva, tears and urine, there is no evidence that HIV can be acquired from these sources. Indeed, HIV infection is not transmitted by touching an infected person; via droplets coughed or sneezed into the air; from sharing utensils such as cups and plates; from swimming pools; from toilet seats; by insects; or by person to person contact in any setting.

In Africa, where heterosexual transmission is the main route of infection, approximately equal numbers of men and women are infected. Many of the women are of childbearing age and paediatric HIV infection is a major problem. It has been estimated by the World Health Organisation (WHO) that in 1987 alone over 20,000 HIV infected infants had been born in Sub-Saharan Africa.[1] On the other hand, in the USA and Europe, where infection in women is predominantly linked to intravenous drug use, about 10 per cent of all cases of AIDS are among women and two per cent among children. There is concern, however, that the heterosexual spread of HIV infection is increasing.

Table 1

Transmission of HIV infection

HIV is spread through:	sexual intercourse;
	infected blood and organ transplants (including semen donation);
	vertical transmission from mother to child.
HIV is not spread through:	insects, food, water, urine, sneezing, coughing, toilets, swimming pools, sweat, tears, shared eating and drinking utensils;
	casual, person to person contact in any setting.

In many countries, reports of AIDS cases are made to a central organisation. In England, Wales and Northern Ireland this is the Communicable Disease Surveillance Centre (CDSC), in Scotland the Communicable Disease (Scotland) Unit (CD(S)U), and in the USA the Centers for Disease Control (CDC). The WHO/EC Surveillance Centre in Paris receives reports from the European region. It has to be emphasised that these reports will underestimate the actual number of people with AIDS because of under-reporting and diagnostic problems; deaths may occur before the definitive diagnosis of AIDS is made.

In Europe, by the end of 1991 more than 65,000 cases of AIDS had been reported, nearly 3,000 of which were in children under 13 years of age.[2] As many as 1,599 of paediatric AIDS cases were from Romania. The majority of these children had acquired infection from infected blood, although in a substantial number the route of infection was unknown. This emphasises the importance of exclusion of blood donors from high risk groups, screening of donated blood and plasma for HIV antibodies, and heat treatment of clotting factor concentrates, along with careful consideration of indications for use of blood products and the use of clean needles and syringes. With these precautions, the relative contribution of infection acquired from blood transfusions or blood products is likely to diminish in the future.

Excluding those cases from Romania, nearly 75 per cent (1050 children) had acquired the infection vertically from their mothers: 44 per cent (464) of these mothers were intravenous drug users.

As AIDS is the end-point of HIV infection, and most adults remain asymptomatic for many years, the estimated number of women with AIDS does not reflect the current HIV epidemic. The prevalence of HIV infection in the population is a more useful indicator, but more difficult to obtain because the vast majority of HIV infected individuals have no signs or symptoms of infection. Estimates are derived from information obtained from special studies based on specific groups which are not necessarily representative of the general population.

Table 2

Exposure Category and Infection Status of HIV Seropositive Children

Reports from the United Kingdom to January 1992

	Infected	Indeterminate	Negative	Total
Mother	133	174	137	444
Haemophilia	238	0	0	238
Blood transfusion	24	0	0	24
Total	395	174	137	706

Provided by Dr Clare Davison, Institute of Child Health, London

In the UK, laboratory reports of confirmed HIV antibody tests for England, Wales and Northern Ireland are notified to the CDSC, and from Scotland to the CD(S)U. The combined reports are published quarterly.[3] However, these figures are likely to underestimate the true prevalence of HIV infection as they only include those individuals who have been tested and testing is not universal. Many infected individuals may not be aware of existing infection or even that they may be, or have been, at increased risk of infection. If testing is selective and depends on identification of risk factors, further bias is introduced. A more accurate estimate of prevalence in the general population is provided by anonymous testing of blood taken for other purposes, although even this is limited to those who need to have their blood taken.[4]

Paediatric HIV and AIDS surveillance in the UK

In addition to the laboratory reporting scheme, paediatricians notify HIV positive children through the British Paediatric Surveillance Unit (BPSU)[5] and these children are followed up so that their infection status can be determined. Cases of AIDS notified to the BPSU are included in the CDSC figures.

By the end of January 1992, 444 children born to HIV infected mothers had been notified from the UK and Eire, and a further 262 children who had received infected blood or blood products were known to be HIV positive (see Table 2). However, not all antibody positive children of HIV infected mothers are HIV infected, since in a number of children under 18 months the presence of HIV antibodies may merely reflect passively acquired maternal antibodies.[6] Of the 444 children born to HIV seropositive mothers, 133 are known to be infected, and 137 are presumed uninfected. The HIV infection status is indeterminate for 174 antibody positive children who are younger than 18 months and who have no other indicator of HIV infection. Ninety three children had been reported with AIDS, 55 of whom were born to HIV positive mothers.

Transmission of HIV infection from mother to child

Vertical transmission of HIV infection can occur before, during or after birth, but in view of the difficulty of making an early diagnosis the relative contribution of each of these routes remains unquantified. Intra-uterine HIV infection can occur; virus has been found in fetal tissue as early as 15 weeks gestation. Virus has also been found in placentas and cord blood. However, since HIV may be present in cervical secretions, and considerable exchange of blood occurs between mother and infant during delivery, acquisition of infection during birth remains a possibility but has not been substantiated. While the relative importance of transmission at delivery is becoming apparent, prospective studies to date do not suggest a difference in risk of infection according to whether the delivery was by caesarian section or vaginal.[7,8] Postnatal transmission of HIV infection following the ingestion of breast milk has been described in several case reports where a breast-feeding mother acquired the infection through a blood transfusion given shortly after the delivery, and the child was subsequently found to be infected.[9] Virus has been found in breast milk. However, in this context, newly acquired maternal infection may pose a greater risk to the foetus or infant. The WHO guidelines[10] discuss the need to balance the benefits of breastfeeding by HIV infected women against the additional risk of transmission through breast milk. The balance of evidence suggests that mothers with established infection can transmit HIV infection through breast milk, although the relative importance of this route remains to be quantified.[11] The additional risk of transmission when a mother was already HIV positive during pregnancy has recently been estimated.[12] Based on a review of prospective studies following children born to HIV infected mothers the increase in the risk of infection in breastfed infants, over and above transmission during pregnancy or at delivery, is estimated to be 14 per cent (95 per cent confidence interval 7–22 per cent).[13]

Diagnosis of HIV infection in children

In adults and older children the diagnosis of HIV infection usually depends on the detection of HIV antibodies in the blood. But in infants the diagnosis is hampered by the fact that maternal antibodies cross the placenta and may persist well into the child's second year of life. All children born to HIV positive women have these antibodies at birth, but only infected children produce their own HIV antibodies. It is extremely difficult to distinguish between the child's own antibodies and the passively acquired maternal antibodies which do not indicate infection in the child. Although most children will lose the passively acquired maternal antibodies by 12 months of age, these may persist for up to 18 months. Therefore, in the absence of other indicators of infection, it is not possible to reach a firm diagnosis of infection before this age nor indeed is it possible to exclude infection in an antibody positive child younger than 18 months.

Although the virus can be isolated in appropriate conditions, these tests are costly and time consuming and not available for routine use. Antigen tests which measure free antigen in the blood are a reliable indication of viral activity; however, antigen is not always detectable, and may reflect progression of disease rather than infection per se. A negative virus of antigen test does not exclude infection. A test which detects and amplifies genetic material of a virus has recently become available in the diagnosis of HIV infection. This test, called the polymerase chain reaction (PCR), still needs careful evaluation and is not yet routinely available for diagnosis.

Rates of vertical transmission and natural history

Estimates of rates of vertical transission vary widely and published estimates from studies where children born to HIV positive women were identified before or at birth and followed until their infection status was determined, range from seven to 39 per cent.[14] Differences in maternal and environmental factors, as well as methods used in calculating the rates, could account for this variation, although currently there is little documented information on factors that influence vertical transmission. The European Collaborative Study (ECS) on children born to HIV positive women reported a rate of vertical transmission of about 15 per cent in a largely asymptomatic population of women, many of whom had a history of intravenous drug use. Transmission was associated with maternal, clinical and immunological status, delivery before 34 weeks gestation and breastfeeding.

The paucity of information on the natural history of paediatric HIV infection is largely due to the difficulty of regular and long-term clinical and laboratory follow-up of children born of HIV infected women and identified at birth. The initial clinical presentation of HIV infection is often non-specific and may involve a wide spectrum of clinical disease, such as generalised swelling of glands, enlarged liver and/or spleen, parotitis, diarrhoea, and fever. More specific symptoms/signs include persistent oral thrush, lymphoid interstitial pneumonitis, lymphomas, opportunistic infections and immunological abnormalities. The period from initial exposure to the onset of AIDS is variable, and in vertically infected infants could be bimodal. In the ECS, about 80 per cent of infected children showed some manifestation of HIV infection by six months. By 12 months, more than one third had developed AIDS or had died of HIV related disease, and the early onset of disease and rapid progression were striking. The rate of progression was much slower after the first year and it is not yet known when, and if, the remaining infected children will develop AIDS. The prognosis after the diagnosis of AIDS is variable and may depend on age at diagnosis and on the presenting symptoms/signs of treatment.[15,16]

Lack of evidence for casual transmission of HIV infection

Information on the lack of casual transmission from children to their close household contacts is accumulating, and there have been no reports of transmission of HIV acquired from children in family, day or foster care settings, or schools.[17,18] Precautions taken to prevent the spread of Hepatitis B virus, which is much more infectious than HIV, are more than adequate to prevent transmission of HIV.[19] Rogers et al[20] tested 89 members of households in which 25 children with HIV infection resided, most of whom were of pre-school age. The household members had close contact with the infected children, and shared many items likely to be soiled with blood and body fluids, such as toys, toothbrushes, eating utensils, toilets and bathtubs. Hugging, kissing, sharing a bed, and bathing together were common. Testing took place at least four months after exposure, and 75 per cent were tested at least a year after exposure. All 89 household members were antibody negative.

No cases of AIDS have been reported among the non-high risk family members of the more than 100,000 AIDS cases reported to the CDC, USA. None of the reported AIDS cases are attributable to exposure to infected persons in the workplace (other than a health care or laboratory setting), day care, or school setting. Friedland et al[21] offer additional evidence for lack of transmission of HIV infection by close casual contact, evaluating 206 household contacts of 90 patents with AIDS. Including the findings from other studies, they report a total of 890 close contacts of 497 index cases and none acquired HIV infection. In a review of the literature, Gershon, Vlahov and Nelson[22] also conclude that the likelihood of non-percutaneous, non-sexual transmission is remote. Further evidence is provided by the ECS on children born to HIV positive women,[23] which failed to confirm earlier reports of seroreversion in two-year-old children, despite follow up of some 80 children beyond the age of three; this implies that infection of children through household contact with their infected mother must be rare since it has not occurred once in 390 person-years observation of antibody negative children.

Concern has been expressed that biting by an infected child could be a possible route of transmission. However, Reed, Shirley and Ross[24] report on the long-term follow up of family members bitten by an HIV infected toddler. All exposed cousins have remained clinically healthy, and antibody was not detected in 20 months of follow up. They also review other reports of biting in individuals infected with HIV and find no evidence of HIV infection acquired through bites, although in two cases where the HIV infected person sustained considerable bleeding in the mouth, transmission of HIV infection through biting did occur through blood rather than saliva.

There is only one well-documented case of infant to mother transmission, where the mother of a chronically ill child with a congenital intestinal abnormality was exposed extensively to her child's body fluids and blood while providing in-hospital nursing care for the child. She did not take precautions to avoid contact with her child's blood and body fluids.[25]

Occupational transmission of HIV infection

The potential for occupational transmission of HIV was appreciated early in the course of the AIDS epidemic, and has been a persistent professional and public health issue since. The risk is dependent on three factors: the probability of infection occurring following a particular incident; the probability of that incident recurring; and the prevalence of HIV infection in the population served. Blood is the only body fluid implicated in occupational HIV infection to date, although this may be a reflection of the low virus load in other body fluids. The risk of infection after parenteral exposure to infected blood is estimated to be approximately 0.4 per cent (95 per cent confidence interval $0.0 - 0.9\%$).[26,27] The risk of infection from mucous membrane exposure or contamination of non-intact skin with HIV infected blood is too low to be quantified in the prospective studies currently under way. Contamination of normal skin with HIV infected blood has not been implicated in HIV transmission, despite the high frequency of this mode of exposure. The same precautions recommended for prevention of Hepatitis B infection are applicable for HIV. Clear guidelines providing advice on the management of blood spills in the school and home setting are available.[28]

Immunisation and HIV infection

The immunological abnormalities associated with HIV infection have raised concerns about immunisation of infected children, especially with live vaccines.[29] However, to date no increase in adverse reactions to immunisations have been reported in HIV infected children, although it appears that immunocompromised and HIV symptomatic children may lose the ability to mount an appropriate and satisfactory response. The WHO recommends routine immunisation of HIV infected children, but withholding BCG vaccination from HIV symptomatic children and from all HIV infected children in areas where prevalence of tuberculosis is low. Substitution of oral polio vaccine for inactivated polio vaccine may be considered for children living in households where someone may be immunosuppressed or have symptomatic HIV infection. Theoretical concerns that immunisation might accelerate the course of the infection are not supported by available evidence.

Conclusion

There has been considerable discussion as to whether children should have their HIV status determined prior to fostering or adoption. This poses diagnostic problems in the infants of mothers of unknown HIV infection status but known to be at high risk. However, in these cases, although a definitive diagnosis of HIV infection is problematic, a blood test could exclude infection. Those found to be antibody positive should be followed up regularly until a definitive diagnosis can be made. With improved management and treatment of HIV related symptoms and signs, early identification of infection in children has now become important. This argument would also pertain in the situation where a child has been sexually abused by someone of known or unknown HIV infection status who is at high risk. However, at the present time, with the relatively low prevalence of HIV infection in the general population, widespread HIV antibody testing of children prior to fostering or adoption would not be advocated, and each case should be considered on its own merit and the likelihood of infection assessed.

References

1 Chin J, 'Current and Future Dimensions of the HIV/AIDS Pandemic in Women and Children', *Lancet*, 336: 221-224, 1990.

2 World Health Organisation, *Aids Surveillance in Europe*, Quarterly report no 32, December 1991.

3 Public Health Laboratory Service, 'AIDS and HIV-1 Antibody reports — United Kingdom', *Communicable Disease Review*, 2; 12: 55-56, 1992.

4 Gill O N, Adler M W, Day N E, 'Monitoring the Prevalence of HIV', *British Medical Journal*, 299: 1295-1298, 1989.

5 Hall S M, Glickman M, 'The British Paediatric Surveillance Unit', *Archives of Diseases in Childhood*, 65: 807-809, 1988.

6 European Collaborative Study, 'Children born to women with HIV-1 infection: natural history and risk of transmission', *Lancet*, 337: 253-260, 1991.

7 Blanche S, Rouzioux C, Guihard Moscato M I, et al, 'A prospective study of infants born to women seropositive for human immunodeficiency virus type 1', *New England Journal of Medicine*, 320: 1643-1648, 1989.

8 European Collaborative Study, 'Risk factors for mother-to-child transmission of HIV-1', *Lancet* 339: 1007-12, 1992.

9 Oxtoby M J, 'Human immunodeficiency virus and other viruses in human milk: placing the issues in broader perspective', *Journal of Paediatric Infectious Diseases*, 7: 825-835, 1988.

10 Global Programme on AIDS. Consensus statement from the WHO/UNICEF constitution on HIV transmission and breastfeeding, Weekly Epidemiological Records, 67: 177-84, 1992.

11 Van de Perre P, Simonon A, Msellati P, et al, 'Postnatal transmission of human immunodefiency virus type 1 from mother to infant: a prospective cohort study in Kigali, Rwanda', *New England Journal of Medicine*, 325: 593-598, 1991.

12 See 8 above.

13 Dunn D T, Newell M L, Ades A E, Peckham C S, 'Risk of Human Immunodeficiency Virus Type 1 Transmission through Breastfeeding',

Lancet 340: 585-88, 1992.

14 Newell M-L, Peckham C S, Lepage P, 'HIV-1 infection in pregnancy: implications for women and children', *AIDS*, 4 (suppl 1): S111-117, 1990.

15 Blanche S, Tardieu M, Duliege A M, et al, 'Longitudinal study of 94 symptomatic infants with perinatally aquired human immunodeficiency virus infection', *American Journal of Diseases in Childhood*, 144: 1210-1215, 1990.

16 Scott G B, Hutto C, Makuch R W, et al, 'Survival in children with perinatally aquired human immunodeficiency virus type 1 infection', *New England Journal of Medicine*, 321: 1791-1796, 1989.

17 Rogers M F, White C R, Sanders R, et al, 'Lack of transmission of human immunodeficiency virus from infected children to their household contacts', *Pediatrics*, 85: 210-214, 1990.

18 Friedland G, Kahl P, Saltzman B, et al, 'Additional evidence for lack of HIV transmission of HIV infection by close interpersonal (casual) contact', *AIDS*, 4: 639-644, 1990.

19 UK Health Department's *Guidance for clinical health care workers: protection against infection with HIV and hepatitis viruses*, HMSO, 1990.

20 See 17 above.

21 See 18 above.

22 Gershon R R M, Vlahov D, Nelson K E, 'The risk of transmission of HIV-1 through non-percutaneous, non-sexual modes: a review', *AIDS*, 4: 645-650, 1990.

23 See 6 above.

24 Shirley L R, Ross S A, 'Risk of transmission of human immunodeficiency virus by bite of an infected toddler', *Paediatrics*, 114: 425-427, 1989.

25 Centres for Disease Control, 'Apparent transmission of HTLV-III/LAV from a child to a mother providing health care', *Morbidity and Mortality Weekly Report*, 35: 76-79, 1986.

26 Gerberding J L, *Risks to health care workers from occupational exposure to hepatitis B virus, human immunodeficiency virus, and cytomegalovirus*, Infectious Diseases Clinics of North America, 3: 734-745, 1989.

27 Henderson D K, Fahay B J, Willy M, et al, 'Risk for occupational transmission of human immundeficiency virus type 1 (HIV-1) associated with clinical exposures', *Annals of internal medicine*, 113: 740-746, 1990.

28 Hanson P J V, Gor D, Jeffries D J, Collins J V, 'Chemical inactivation of HIV on surfaces', *British Medical Journal*, 298: 862-864, 1989.

29 Onorato I M, Markowitz L E, Oxtoby M J, 'Childhood immunisation, vaccine-preventable diseases and infection with human immunodeficiency virus', *Pediatric Infectious Diseases*, 6: 588-595, 1988.

3 HIV seropositive babies:
Implications in planning for their future

Dr Jacqueline Mok, MD, FRCP(ED)

Dr Jacqueline Mok is a Consultant Paediatrician (Community Child Health) responsible for the surveillance and management of children born to HIV infected mothers in Edinburgh and the Lothians. Edinburgh is the only centre in the United Kingdom from which children have been recruited for the multicentre European Collaborative Study on mother-to-child transmission of HIV infection.

In the United Kingdom about 13 per cent of patients reported to be HIV antibody positive have injecting drug use (IDU) identified as a risk activity. The situation in Scotland, however, is different: fifty one per cent of those reported to be HIV positive have been associated with IDU.[1,2] About 60 per cent of the recent Scottish reports originate from Edinburgh, and reinforce earlier studies which revealed more frequent needle sharing amongst IDUs in Edinburgh compared with those in Glasgow or South London. When HIV was introduced into Edinburgh in 1983, it spread rapidly.[3] It is estimated that in Edinburgh, one in a hundred men aged between 15 and 44 years, and one in 250 women of childbearing age are infected with the virus.[4,5] Unlike many centres in the UK where HIV has primarily infected the male homosexual population, the problems seen in Edinburgh have involved heterosexual transmission between men and women, as well as vertical transmission from mother to child. The relatively long incubation period of HIV infection means that relatively few AIDS cases have been reported for Scotland so far, but just over half of the AIDS deaths in Scotland had occurred during 1989/1990.

The Paediatric Counselling and Screening Clinic
The setting up of an open access screening and counselling clinic at the Edinburgh City Hospital in October 1985 facilitated the identification of

HIV seropositive pregnant women. By December 1985, seven infants had been born, necessitating the co-ordination of paediatric surveillance, and in January 1986, the paediatric counselling and screening clinic was established specifically for 'at risk' infants and their families.[6] To date, some 75 families have been enrolled in this clinic, with 90 infants born to 73 seropositive women. The cumulative numbers of infants being monitored are shown in Figure 1.

Figure 1 **Infants of HIV+ mothers – cumulative total**

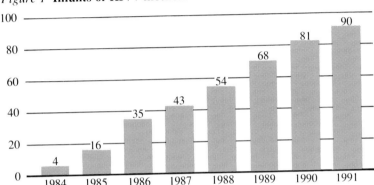

The clinic is one of ten centres participating in the European Collaborative Study to evaluate the risk of mother–child transmission of HIV and study the natural history of vertically acquired HIV infection.[7,8] The paediatric clinic is held in conjunction with the adult HIV screening and counselling clinic, and is staffed by a consultant paediatrician, a paediatric registrar and a health visitor; the model is that of a family clinic, with children being seen along with their parent(s). Close liaison exists between the paediatric staff and medical staff responsible for the parents' health care. The majority of referrals come from the adult physicians who are already monitoring the health of many HIV seropositive women, and other referrals come from antenatal clinics throughout the city, neonatal and general paediatricians, general practitioners, health visitors and social workers. The surveillance procedure is outlined in Table 1 overleaf. Inpatient facilities are available at the Regional Infectious Diseases Unit of the City Hospital where admission is under the care of the consultant paediatrician, thereby maintaining continuity of care.

Table 1

Surveillance programme for infants born to HIV seropositive women

Follow-up of the child	Regular review 1-3 monthly for growth, development and signs of HIV infection
	Discuss who needs to know
	Ensure mother understands lines of referral if child becomes unwell
	Discuss child care issues, including immunisation
	Monitor laboratory results
	Liaise with social work and education staff, if necessary
Referral if necessary to	Adult physician
	Drug services
	Voluntary agencies/self help groups
	Social work department

The mothers

In Edinburgh, evidence of HIV infection in pregnancy has so far been found almost exclusively in women who have been injecting drug users or whose partners are known to be HIV seropositive due to injecting drug use.[9] These women tend to live in areas of the city with multiple deprivation, where other factors predispose to adverse pregnancy outcome, rather than HIV infection per se.[10] Pregnant women with HIV infection often want advice about the risks of passing the virus to the child, the outlook for an infected child, as well as the likelihood of pregnancy affecting their own HIV disease. On theoretical grounds, pregnancy might be expected to increase the risk of progression from an asymptomatic state to active disease. Initial studies suggested that following pregnancy, there was a high incidence of progression to AIDS.[11,12] However, the mothers in those studies were identified because they had already delivered a child with AIDS, and thus represented the severe end of the spectrum. In Edinburgh, the monitoring of a cohort of asymptomatic HIV infected women has revealed no differences in clinical status or laboratory parameters between women who had no pregnancies and those who had pregnancies following seroconversion.

It is important that women with HIV infection be given the opportunity to discuss issues surrounding vertical transmission, and one of the paediatricians should meet the woman in the antenatal period to do so. Some women decide to terminate their pregnancy while others choose to continue. For the latter, the purpose and nature of follow-up for the child should be explained, and permission obtained to enrol the child into the study. The mother and child should be seen within the first week, and the infant must be examined by a paediatrician. Blood is taken for evaluation of immune function and virological status. Future visits are then arranged, either at the clinic or in the family home; about 80 per cent of children are seen at home. The frequency of appointments for reviews at the clinic is shown in Figure 2.

Figure 2 **Number of appointments**

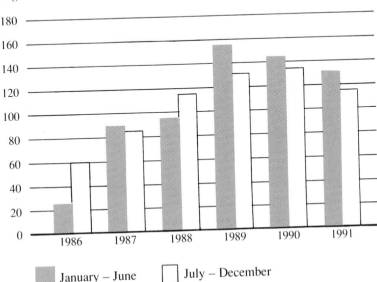

January – June   July – December

Perinatal care

The unpredictable lifestyles and low level of antenatal care amongst pregnant HIV seropositive women have led to anxieties about premature deliveries and low birth weight babies with the attendant problems. While it is unlikely that an infant would be born with AIDS, infants born to seropositve women have to be assumed to be at high risk of infection. Fears, both perceived and real, among medical and nursing staff at the clinic were discussed in detail during several meetings and guidelines drawn up. It was decided that seropositve women should deliver wherever they were booked, ie no maternity unit was to be singled out for these deliveries. In view of the large quantities of blood and amniotic fluid present, appropriate precautions during the delivery were to include impermeable protective clothing and safety spectacles and gloves. Ideally, the infant should be bathed in the labour ward to wash off traces of blood. Care should be taken to avoid chilling the newborn. The well infant is kept in the same room as the mother, while isolation facilities with specifically identified equipment are available for the pre-term or ill infant needing special care.

Clinical spectrum of HIV infection

Earlier reports which document the clinical manifestations and immunological abnormalities of paediatric HIV infection have concentrated on the more severely affected infants.[13,14] The mortality of children with AIDS is high, but the ultimate progress of less severely affected children, or asymptomatic children, is unknown. Prospective studies currently in progress are observing a bimodal distribution in the severity of clinical disease. The European Collaborative Study reported that approximately one third of HIV infected children will develop AIDS, severe symptoms related to HIV, or will die within the first year of life. The remaining two thirds of the children will survive beyond the second year, follow a milder course and may even become asymptomatic in early childhood.[15] Retrospective reviews of large cohorts of children confirm the bimodal picture, and allow clinical prognostic markers to be established.[16] An indicator disease of pneumocystis carinii pneumonia and presentation in the first year of life have been shown to be independent and important indices of poor outcome. A diagnosis of lymphoid interstitial pneumonitis, on the other hand, has been associated with low mortality and survival into later childhood.

Table 2 (below) shows the classification system for paediatric HIV infection, as proposed by the Centers for Disease Control, Atlanta, USA.[17] It highlights the fact that every system can be affected by the virus, either directly or indirectly. In the early stages of infection, many children present with findings which cannot be directly attributable to HIV infection, viz, recurrent fever, failure to thrive, generalised lymphadenopathy, hepatosplenomegaly or persistent diarrhoea. Many of these signs and symptoms can be found in the absence of HIV infection, especially in children from socio-economically deprived areas.

Table 2

Classification of HIV infection in children

P0	Indeterminate status		
P1	Infected but asymptomatic children		
P2	Symptomatic disease		
	A	Non-specific findings	
	B	Progressive neurological disease	
	C	Lymphoid interstitial pneumonitis	
	D	Secondary infectious diseases:	
		D1	Opportunistic infections
		D2	Recurrent serious bacterial infections
		D3	Other infectious diseases
	E	Secondary cancers	
	F	Other diseases possibly due to HIV, eg, cardiopathy, nephopathy	

Neurological diseases, including neurodevelopmental abnormalities, have been reported to occur in 20–90 per cent of children infected with

HIV.[18,19,20] HIV infection of the brain presents with developmental delay or regression, failure of brain growth and abnormalities in muscle tone and power. Features of cerebral palsy develop, and these may be accompanied by impairment of cognitive function and seizures. The degree of debility varies as does the course, which may be static, rapidly progressive or intermittent in progression with periods where symptoms plateau. Lymphoid interstitial pneumonitis (LIP) is the most frequent pulmonary disease associated with paediatric HIV infection. The onset is insidious, with cough and breathlessness on exertion. With progressive lung involvement, the child may be oxygen dependent and severely limited in his or her activities.

Secondary infectious diseases include opportunistic infections, the most common of which is pneumocystis carinii pneumonia. This presents suddenly, usually with fever and breathlessness. Oral thrush may disseminate into the oesophagus, resulting in anorexia and weight loss. Children with HIV infection present with a greater frequency of bacterial infections, compared to adults. There is some evidence that HIV infected children are more prone to viral upper respiratory infections.[21]

Kaposi's sarcoma, the hallmark of AIDS in homosexual men, is very rare in HIV infected children. With increased survival, other tumours, eg, lymphoma are being reported and it remains to be seen whether the increased incidence of tumours is the result of therapeutic intervention, or merely a reflection of the natural history of the disease. Improved survival will also result in other manifestations being observed, such as involvement of the heart, kidneys and liver. Again, difficulties will arise in unravelling the cause and effect of therapy.

Medical management of the infected child

To test or not to test
The clinical spectrum of HIV infection in children can be non-specific and overlap with those of other common childhood illnesses. The clinician should therefore have a high index of suspicion, especially in areas of high prevalence of HIV infection.

Epidemiological information which warrants HIV testing in a child includes the following:

- Known HIV infection in mother;
- Mother with known risk activity, such as IDU;
- Mother is sexual partner of IDU, bisexual or HIV infected man;
- Recipient of blood and blood products prior to universal donor screening (October 1985 in UK);
- Mother with repeated episodes of sexually transmitted diseases;
- History of child sexual abuse;
- Sexually promiscuous adolescent;
- Adolescent IDU.

Clinical features suggestive of HIV infection are listed in Table 2 above, and should again alert the clinician to HIV testing. When HIV infection is suspected because of family or social history or clinical findings, the child and both parents should be tested simultaneously whenever possible. Because of the stigma of the diagnosis of HIV infection, most clinicians are uncomfortable with discussing the issues which surround testing. Indeed, previous guidelines were against testing, in view of the dire social consequences and the lack of a definitive cure for the disease. Over the last two years, however, much more information has been gathered about the treatments available. In many centres, HIV testing is encouraged to permit early identification of those children who are infected so that therapeutic options can be offered.

Prior to testing, the paediatrician should explain the nature and purpose of the test; the nature of HIV infection; confidentiality of the test results and the likely problems with discrimination should the result be disclosed; the implications of a positive test result for the child as well as the birth parent/s; and the potential medical benefits of early intervention with prophylactic medications for asymptomatic children.

Test results should always be presented in person, and never by letter or telephone. In addition to revealing the result, the therapeutic options should be presented and appropriate referral made to support services. The family should be informed about the need to disclose the child's infectious status to medical personnel during emergency consultations, to enable the appropriate therapy to be given.

Asymptomatic carrier
A proportion of infected children will remain asymptomatic although

they are infectious. They and their families need help in living with the stigma and social isolation brought on by being HIV seropositive. It is likely that the child would have been infected through the mother so that at least one, if not both, parents will be infected. Other children in the household may or may not be similarly infected, but will certainly require counselling and support.

The young child with asymptomatic HIV infection should be allowed to lead a normal life. This involves attending school and taking part in all activities. The rights of the child and family to confidentiality must be respected, and this could mean the family choosing not to disclose the child's HIV status to any member of the social work, health care or teaching staff. The fear of being stigmatised, or of other children being withdrawn from the school, will understandably lead to several HIV affected families not disclosing that information. Moreover, as clear evidence is emerging that HIV infection is not transmitted through casual contact within the day care, school or work setting, it could be argued that teachers and schoolmates do not need to know.

Healthy carriers, when approaching adolescence, will have to be counselled on the implications of their disease. This has to start with healthy living and avoidance of activities, such as injecting drug use, which will contribute to the development of full-blown AIDS. Adolescents will require support when embarking on relationships with either sex and should be encouraged to adopt a responsible attitude. They may also feel anger towards their parent, who will be blamed for their HIV status, fear about their own future, and guilt and anxiety that they might be responsible for passing the infection to their partner or offspring. With the adoption of safer sex practices there will also come the realisation that they may never be able to have children.

The symptomatic child
Chronic ill-health: The incubation period of HIV in children is shorter than that reported in adults. Prior to the diagnosis of AIDS, many children will present with chronic ill-health. Infants and young children with HIV infection may have recurrent severe infections, protracted diarrhoea, failure to gain weight as well as neurological complications necessitating recurrent hospitalisations. While the diarrhoea may be difficult to treat,

the debilitated child will require medical and nursing care because of dehydration and malnutrition. Regular intravenous infusions of immunoglobulin have been shown to alleviate recurrent bacterial infections.[22,23]

Good nutrition is vital for HIV infected children to maintain optimal growth. Advice from a paediatric dietitian is essential, although some low-income families may be unable to comply with the recommendations. Infectious complications or malabsorption due to HIV infection of the gastrointestinal tract may necessitate parenteral feeding. Although this has to be initiated in hospital, some families may be able to cope at home with the support of community nurses.

Neurological disease could progress rapidly and lead to a physically disabled child with loss of intellect. Such children will make demands on facilities for disabled children which are presently over-stretched. The use of zidovudine (AZT) has proved beneficial in children with brain involvement.[24] However, there remains a dilemma as to when and at what dose zidovudine should be started for HIV infected children. A multicentre European trial was commenced in September 1992, with the aim of comparing early versus deferred use of zidovudine in children born to HIV infected women.

Preparing children for death: Children who are old enough will start to ask questions about their future and about the effects of HIV disease on their life, especially if they have had several hospital admissions and endured painful treatments. The majority of adults feel uncomfortable when faced with the question 'Am I going to die?' from a child. Those looking after ill children will need to be prepared for such questions and be able to answer them truthfully, appropriately and with sympathy.

The present state of knowledge is that no cure is effective against HIV although many aspects of the disease, eg infection and malnutrition, can be treated. At some stage, when all therapy has failed, the carers may wish to take the child home for terminal care. Although such a wish has to be respected, the carers must also consider the effects on the other members of the family when a terminally ill child is nursed at home. It must be remembered that HIV disease is a disease of the family unit. In many cases the child will be diagnosed first, then the mother and other members of the close family who may become ill simultaneously. In such cases, the stress inflicted on other relatives can be very severe.

Bereavement support for the family: Parents, siblings, members of the wider family as well as medical and nursing and social work staff will all need to be supported following the death of the child. Feelings of relief, guilt, anger and fear may be very real, especially if any of the family members is similarly infected. Referral to professionals trained in bereavement counselling may help.

The HIV affected family

Most cases of paediatric AIDS are due to vertical transmission. Often, one or both parents are also affected. In some families, there may be more than one infected child. The uninfected siblings are by no means unaffected by the AIDS virus, as they experience illness and death in the family. Grandparents, if involved, will also have to mourn the loss of younger generations (children and grandchildren) from AIDS. Throughout the world millions of 'AIDS orphans' are anticipated in the 1990s, and social services will have to be prepared to care for these children.[25]

Integration into the community

Not all parents will be able to care for their infected child: continued drug use in the parents may lead to inconsistent child care, or ill health may preclude them from caring for the child. Consequently, alternative child care arrangements may have to be found. All child carers (foster carers, day carers, nursery nurses, teachers) should receive in-service training on HIV infection, with emphasis on the low infectivity of the virus, the known routes of transmission and the practical aspects of good hygiene. It is not always possible to identify all infected children; stringent standards of hygiene should be applied universally in all child care establishments.

As HIV infected children reach school age, educational institutions should be prepared to integrate these children into mainstream schools. Headteachers are charged with the responsibility of educating staff, parents and children on the general information surrounding HIV and AIDS. Clear guidelines have been set for headteachers in schools in the

Lothians, stressing the importance of treating HIV infected children normally and sensitively.[26] Information about specific children should remain confidential: it is always prudent to ask 'Who needs to know and why?'

Conclusion

The infected child comes from an HIV affected family, demanding the care and co-ordination of multiple services. The degree to which maternal illness affects the parenting ability must always be assessed, and consideration given to the welfare of the uninfected children in the family. Figure 3 attempts to predict the outcome of infants born to HIV seropositive women. It is not unreasonable to expect that some infants will have escaped HIV infection, but infants may need to be monitored until adolescence before they can be declared free from infection.

Figure 3 **The Future**

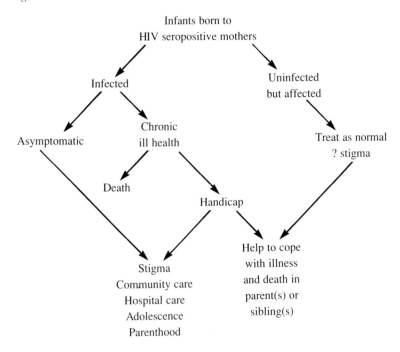

The lack of an available cure or vaccination against HIV does not necessarily mean that nothing can be done for HIV infected individuals. Infants of HIV seropositive women present tremendous and complex challenges to medical, nursing, social work and education professionals, as well as to members of voluntary agencies. A high degree of collaboration between community and hospital services is required. The importance of a multi-disciplinary team approach is highlighted, especially in managing sick children and their families. Current prejudicial attitudes towards homosexual men and drug abusers will have to change and it must be remembered that HIV infection is no longer confined to 'risk groups'. Finally, research into vaccines and cures for HIV must be supported so that the prognosis for infected individuals can be improved.

References

1 Communicable Disease Report, *AIDS and HIV-1 infection in the United Kingdom*: monthly report, January 1992.

2 AIDS News Supplement, CDS Weekly Report, Communicable Diseases (Scotland) Unit, 1 February 1992.

3 Brettle R P, Bisset K, Burns S, et al, 'HIV and drug misuse: the Edinburgh experience', *British Medical Journal*, 295: 421-424, 1987.

4 Scottish Home and Health Department, *Report of the national working party on health service implications of HIV infection*, Edinburgh, 1987.

5 Johnstone F D, MacCallum L, Brettle R, et al, 'Testing for HIV in pregnancy, three year experience in Edinburgh City', *Scottish Medical Journal* 34: 561-563, 1989.

6 Mok J Y Q, Hague R A, Taylor R F, et al, 'The management of children born to HIV seropositive women', *Journal of Infection*, 18: 119-124, 1989.

7 European Collaborative Study, 'Mother-to-child transmission of HIV infection', *Lancet* ii: 1039-1042, 1988.

8 European Collaborative Study, 'Children born to women with HIV-1 infection: natural history and risk of transmission', *Lancet* 337: 253-260, 1991.

9   See 5 above.

10 Johnstone F D, MacCallum L, Brettle R P, et al, 'Does infection with HIV affect the outcome of pregnancy?' *British Medical Journal*, 296: 467, 1988.

11 Scott G B, Fischl M A, Klimas N, et al, *Mothers of infants with the acquired immunodeficiency syndrome*, JAMA, 253: 363-366, 1985.

12 Minkoff H, Nanda D, Menez R, Fiking S, 'Pregnancies resulting in infants with AIDS or ARC: follow-up of mothers, children and subsequently born siblings', *Obstet Gynecol*, 69: 288-291, 1987.

13 Rubinstein A, Sticklick M, Gupta A, et al, *Acquired immunodeficiency with reversed T4/T8 ratio in infants born to promiscuous and drug addicted mothers*, JAMA, 249: 1350-1356, 1983.

14 Scott G B, Buck B E, Leterman JG, et al, 'Acquired immunodeficiency syndrome in infants', *New England Journal of Medicine*, 310: 76-81, 1984.

15 See 8 above.

16 Scott G B, Hutto C, Makuch R W, et al, 'Survival in children with perinatally acquired HIV type 1 infection', *New England Journal of Medicine*, 321: 1791-1796, 1989.

17 Centers for Disease Control, 'Classification system for HIV infection in children under 13 years of age', *MMWR*, 36: 225-235, 1987.

18 European Collaborative Study, 'Neurologic signs in young children with HIV infection', *Paediatric Infectious Diseases Journal* 6: 402-406, 1990.

19 Belman A L, Diamond G, Dickson D, Llena J, Lantos G, Rubinstein A, 'Paediatric AIDS', *American Journal of Diseases in Childhood* 142: 29-35, 1988.

20 Epstein L G, Leroy R, Sharer L R, et al, 'Neurological manifestations of HIV infection', *Paediatrics* 78: 678-687, 1986.

21 Hague R A, Burns S E, Hargreaves F D, Mok J Y Q, Yap P L, 'Virus infections of the respiratory tract in HIV infected children', *Journal of Infectious Diseases* 24: 31-36, 1992.

22 Hague R A, Yap P L, Mok J Y Q, et al, 'Intravenous immunoglobulin in HIV infection: evidence for the efficacy of treatment', *Archives of Diseases in Childhood* 64: 1146-1150, 1989.

23 The National Institute of Child Health and Human Development Intravenous Immunoglobulin Study Group, 'Intravenous immune globulin for the prevention of bacterial infections in children with symptomatic human immunodeficiency virus infection', *New England Journal of Medicine* 325(2): 73-80, 1991.

24 Pizzo P A, Eddy J, Falloon J, et al, 'Effect of continuous intravenous infusion zidovudine (AZT) in children with symptomatic HIV infection', *New England Journal of Medicine* 319: 799-896, 1988.

25 Mok J, Editorial, 'HIV infection in children', *British Medical Journal* 302: 921-922, 1991.

26 Lothian Regional Council Department of Education, *Children who are HIV+ or have AIDS – Guidelines to Head Teachers*, Edinburgh, 1990.

4 Children looked after away from home:
Some legal implications

Simmy Viinikka

Simmy Viinikka, a solicitor, works at the Terrence Higgins Trust. She was formerly a solicitor in an inner London borough adoption agency and employed in private practice.

This chapter discusses some of the legal issues which may be relevant in the context of the placement of children at risk of HIV infection in substitute families. It looks in some detail at the issue of consent to testing, and goes on to examine briefly key legal issues for children infected with HIV who are being looked after by a local authority or voluntary organisation. This task is made both more daunting and more straightforward as a result of the implementation of the Children Act in October 1991. Despite the large amount of relevant guidance,[1] regulations and policy documents produced by the Department of Health and many local authorities, ambiguities and occasional unforeseen consequences are emerging as the Act is put into practice. Nevertheless the clear and explicit philosophy behind the Act and its thorough and comprehensive nature should eventually lead to greater simplicity and certainty in a hitherto very difficult area of the law.

Note for readers in Scotland and Northern Ireland

Readers in Northern Ireland will be aware that their legal system is much the same as that of England and Wales. The law relating to children is similar in substance, but readers should note that statutes and regulations affecting Northern Ireland may differ in nomenclature, commencement dates and procedural details. Where known, these are provided in the text. The provisions of the Children Act, with possible modifications, are expected to come into force in Northern Ireland in 1993.

Scottish law and the Scottish legal system are significantly and materially different. For example, the Children Act 1989 does not apply to Scotland (except for minor provisions). Children's matters in Scotland are dealt with under the Social Work (Scotland) Act 1968 and through the Children's Panel system. English case law, such as the Gillick decision, is not binding in Scotland but may be persuasive if referred to in an individual case. The 1981 and 1986 Education Acts do not apply in Scotland where there are, for example, no school governors in state schools.

Scottish readers cannot therefore rely on this chapter for an account of the law. However, it is likely that a Scottish court would adopt a similar approach to a case involving children and HIV and readers may therefore find the general comments on HIV and the law of interest.

HIV testing and medical treatment

The right to consent: children and young persons
Children and young people under the age of 18 have limited legal powers. Consent to medical treatment must normally be given by a parent or guardian on behalf of a child. However, a young person of 16 and over can consent to 'any surgical, medical or dental treatment which, in the absence of consent, would constitute a trespass to the person' (S.8, Family Law Reform Act, 1969; S.4, Age of Majority Act [NI] 1969). It should be noted here that section 8 refers to 'treatment', so that any medical procedures would need to be therapeutic. The section does not apply where a young person lacks the mental capacity to consent when the consent of the parent or guardian must be sought. Leave of the court will be required where a proposed treatment is non-therapeutic (*re E (a minor)* 1991). It has recently been held that section 8 does not confer complete autonomy on a young person in that a refusal to consent to treatment may be overridden by the court. This decision followed a similar line of reasoning to *re R* (see below), and concerned a young woman who refused treatment for an anorexic condition. Treatment was ordered (*re J (a minor)* 1992).

The legal position regarding those under 16 was given extensive consideration by the House of Lords in the Gillick case in 1985 (*Gillick v West Norfolk & Wisbech Area Health Authority*) and was partially reviewed in 1991 (*re R (a minor)*).

The Gillick case concerned an application to the court by a mother who wanted to ensure that contraceptive facilities would not be made available to her daughters, who were all under 16, without her consent. The court held that provided a young person is, in the doctor's opinion, of sufficient maturity to understand what is proposed and to make up his or her own mind, she or he is entitled to consent to medical treatment despite being under 16. Accordingly a young person under 16 may in certain circumstances lawfully consent to undergo an HIV antibody test without parental or other consent. Two qualifications to this are set out in the Gillick decision. Firstly, treatment without parental knowledge is exceptional, and it is the doctor's duty in every case to try and persuade the young person to allow his or her parents to be informed. Secondly, the young person has to be seen to understand not only the medical advice offered but, where relevant, its wider social and moral implications in order to give fully informed consent. For example, a young person who can lawfully consent to the setting of a broken arm may lack the capacity to give valid consent to an HIV antibody test. The Gillick decision is given statutory recognition in the Children Act where a court, when making an emergency protection or child assessment order, or an interim care or supervision order, may direct that a child be psychiatrically or medically examined. The child, if of sufficient understanding, may refuse such an examination (ss 38 (6), 43(8), 44(7)).

Regrettably, the decision of the Court of Appeal in *re R (a minor)* has reopened the debate at a time when the 'Gillick' principle seemed to be settled in law. *Re R* was concerned with the medical treatment of a 15-year-old girl with psychiatric problems. At least one of the judges in *re R* appears to have held that, whilst a child with sufficient capacity may consent to treatment, if he or she vetoes it, treatment may nevertheless lawfully be given with the consent of a parent, guardian, or local authority if the child is in care. This flies in the face of the spirit of the Children Act and of the Gillick decision itself, where Lord Scarman said that 'as a matter of law the parental right to determine whether or not their minor children below the age of 16 will have medical treatment terminates if and when the child achieves sufficient understanding and intelligence to enable him or her to understand what is proposed.' *Re R* has cast doubt on this principle, and a further House of Lords decision is needed to restate the law.

The law concerning consent to testing and treatment for babies and young children who do not have sufficient capacity to consent on their own behalf, is unchanged by the Gillick debate but has been considerably revised by the Children Act. Consent to testing in all such cases must be given by a person with *parental responsibility*.

Parental responsibility is a new legal concept which is defined to include all the rights, duties, powers, responsibilities and authority which, by law, a parent of a child has in relation to the child and his or her property (S.3, Children Act). Parental responsibility extends to the child's mother in every case and to the father if married to the mother or if acquired by a court order or a formal agreement. A person caring for a child under a *residence order* and a local authority (or voluntary organisation) looking after a child who is in care under a *care order* will also have parental responsibility during the currency of the order. Where a parent has asked a local authority to provide accommodation for a child (previously known as reception into care), the local authority does not acquire parental responsibility.

Local authorities and consent

Whether a local authority may consent to testing or treatment on behalf of a child therefore depends on whether or not it has parental responsibility for that child. It is important to note that the parent of a child in care does not lose his or her parental responsibility on the making of a care order and may continue to exercise it provided that he or she does not do so in a way which is incompatible with the terms of any order. In theory, such a parent could arrange an HIV antibody test for his or her child in care. A local authority may act to limit the exercise of parental responsibility if it considers that to do so is in the interests of the welfare of the child (S. 33(3)(b) Children Act).

Any decision to test a child in care for HIV infection must be made by a local authority in the context of its general duty under section 22(3) of the Act to safeguard and promote the welfare of the child. A local authority is also subject to new legal duties to have due regard to the child's religious, racial, cultural and linguistic background and to ascertain the wishes and feelings of the child, his or her parents and any other person who has parental responsibility or whose wishes and feelings the authority considers to be relevant. In order to fulfil properly all these duties, and in the absence of a medical emergency, it would appear desirable for any decision to seek an HIV antibody test to be made at a statutory review or case conference (even if the result of the test is not to be reported back to the decision-making group.) Review procedure is governed by the Review of Children's Cases Regulations 1991. Notwithstanding its obligation to consult, the ultimate decision to test a child in its care rests with the local authority. The Children Act reinforces the well-established principle whereby the wardship jurisdiction cannot normally be invoked to interfere with the local authority's exercise of its discretion in relation to the upbringing of a child in its care (*A* v *Liverpool City Council 1982*).

The Arrangements for Placement of Children (General) Regulations 1991 provide for the medical examination and the preparation of a written assessment of the state of health of every child who is looked after by a local authority or voluntary organisation. In arranging a placement, a local authority is to have regard to a wide range of considerations in respect of the child's state of health and health history. A local authority could, subject to its duty to safeguard and promote the welfare of such children, decide (provided that it has the consent of those with parental responsibility) to test for HIV under these regulations. However, it is not the present policy of BAAF (British Agencies for Adoption & Fostering) nor of any local authority to arrange screening for HIV of *all* children being looked after.

Limits to parental powers
A parent, in consenting to testing or medical treatment on behalf of a child in respect of whom he or she has parental responsibility, is not subject to the statutory duty of the local authority to *safeguard and promote* the child's welfare. However, a parent has nevertheless an enforceable legal duty when making a decision on behalf of a child, to do so in accordance with the interests of the welfare of that child. This duty was discussed in the Gillick case and was confirmed in *Re B (a minor) 1991*. This was a case where the mother of a 12-year-old girl

refused to allow her to have an abortion and the local authority made the child a ward of court. The court granted leave for the abortion, holding that the interests of the ward were first and paramount and therefore the wishes of the mother could not be said to be conclusive.

A clear analogy can be made to a situation where there is a dispute as to whether or not a child should have an HIV test. Such a dispute could arise where a local authority is accommodating a child at the request of the child's parents, and therefore does not have parental responsibility for that child. The local authority, or any other interested party, may apply to the court under section 8 of the Children Act for a *specific issue order* to resolve the question. Any person who can demonstrate a sufficient interest in the child's welfare, may, as an alternative, apply to make the child a ward of court, and wardship may also be appropriate where there is a dispute over the child's capacity to make a decision (*re R*). Wardship is not available in respect of children in care but a local authority may apply with leave of the court for the exercise of the High Court's inherent jurisdiction in specific cases of dispute or difficulty. It is for the person with parental responsibility for a young child to decide whether and when the child is to be told of his or her antibody status. The issue has arisen in practice in the cases of haemophiliac children with HIV whose parents have taken various attitudes towards telling their children, and health professionals and social workers have had to respect these views. A serious dispute may be brought before the court as described above.

Confidentiality and access to information

The medical context

A doctor treating a child or young person is bound by the same professional and legal obligations of confidentiality which protect adult patients. In the majority of cases, a parent will give consent for a child to be tested and he or she will also be given the result. However, where a young person over 16, or younger if sufficiently mature, has an HIV test and will not tell his or her parents or allow a doctor to do so, his or her wish should be respected (Gillick).

The medical duty of confidentiality is not absolute. Disclosure may be required by statute or in court proceedings, and may also be justified on public interest grounds, for example, in the investigation of serious crime.

The General Medical Council revised its guidance on professional confidence in November 1991; what was previously described as a *duty* to disclose information regarding suspected child abuse to a third party is now only a *discretion* to do so.[2] Disclosure may only take place in 'exceptional circumstances' and a doctor must be prepared to justify disclosure in each case. The practical implications of this shift are not yet apparent.

A court will hear evidence given in breach of the doctor's duty of confidentiality if it finds that the public interest in disclosure outweighs the professional duty of confidence. This happened in *re C (a minor) 1991*, an adoption application where a doctor volunteered evidence of the mother's medical condition without her consent, and in *W v Egdell*, which concerned an adult psychiatric patient.

There has been considerable debate about whether a doctor has the power or indeed the duty to disclose a young person's antibody positive status to a sexual partner or other third party. In making such a decision a doctor must consider whether there is a serious and identifiable risk of infection to the third party, whether the young person could be persuaded to tell the third party him or herself, and assess the risk in the context of any agreement to adopt safer sex. If the third party is also the doctor's patient it could be argued that the doctor is not merely empowered to disclose, but that he or she may have a legal duty to do so. There are so far no decided cases in England and Wales on this point, and a doctor facing this situation risks being held in breach of his or her professional and legal duty of confidence if he or she wrongly discloses, although the 'public interest' argument may succeed. On the other hand, practitioners in the USA have been successfully sued for negligence outside the AIDS context where they maintained confidentiality and did not disclose to a third party (*Tarasoff* v *Regents of the University of California 1976*). Unauthorised disclosure to family and household members cannot easily be justified, as the risk of HIV transmission through ordinary casual contact is so slight as to be almost negligible.

Individuals have the right of access to medical records held about them compiled after 1 November 1991 by virtue of the Access to Health

Records Act 1991. In the case of young children, parents may have access to this information on their behalf.

The local authority context

Social services departments in many districts have developed policy on dealing with HIV/AIDS stressing the need for confidentiality. Model guidance has been prepared by the Local Authority Association[3] and draft guidelines on children and HIV, which consider confidentiality in some detail, have been published by the Department of Health in July 1992.

A local authority or voluntary organisation looking after a child has a duty of confidentiality in respect of the affairs of that child. Regulations provide for the maintenance of comprehensive records in respect of each child being looked after by a local authority. Such records are normally to be retained for a period of 75 years from the child's birth and steps should be taken to ensure their safe-keeping and to restrict access to them to authorised persons. Individuals have the right of access to their case files under the Access to Personal Files Act 1987 and the Access to Personal Files (Social Services) Regulations 1989. Because of the particularly sensitive nature of this information, some local authorities have taken steps to ensure that information relating to a child's HIV status is kept off the case file and retained separately at Assistant Director or equivalent level.

A local authority or voluntary organisation is obliged to enter into a 'foster placement agreement' in respect of each child whom it is arranging to place with a foster parent. This agreement must include a statement containing all the information which the authority considers necessary to enable foster parents to care for the child and, in particular, information regarding the child's state of health and need for health care and surveillance. Where any significant information is withheld, the reason should be recorded on the child's case file. It seems to me that a foster carer should therefore be given all information available to the local authority about a child's HIV status and any known risk factors. Foster carers are required to treat any information so given to them as confidential and should receive training on the maintenance of confidentiality and the safe-keeping of documentation relating to a child.

Policy and good practice regarding disclosure have developed over time and will continue to do so. For example, in Lothian where there are a number of HIV positive children in foster care, social services were initially advised that the parents of other children should be told when an HIV positive child came into a foster family. This advice has now been rescinded. In Lothian and most other areas, disclosure of antibody status is restricted initially to a very limited number of people within the social services department and the child's primary health and general care givers only. Any disclosure has to be justified in accordance with the council's policy on what is termed a 'need to know' basis.

The National Foster Care Association's advice is that any disclosure should be authorised by the child's social worker on a similar basis. In most cases it advises that there is no 'need to know' in the case of a healthy child where schools, nurseries and other organisations operate a good general standard of hygiene. This considerably reduces the need for their principals and staff to be told of an individual child's status. Department of Education and Science (DES) guidelines[4] emphasise the reduction of risk through good hygiene, the need for confidentiality and the possibility of discrimination against a child whose antibody positive status becomes known.

However, the need to know can be interpreted extremely widely and contrary to popular belief does not eliminate the need for consent prior to disclosure. In some cases other considerations may prevail, for example, a social services department may decide to breach confidentiality for child welfare reasons if a known HIV positive child in care is having a sexual relationship with another child also being looked after by the authority. The department would have to consider, among other factors, the other child's antibody status if known, the positive child's knowledge and practice of safer sex, the parents' and the young person's own wishes. In legal terms the authority must balance its duty to safeguard and promote the welfare of both children with its duty of care towards those, including the second child, who might have a claim against it for negligence if it does not disclose, and its duty of confidence towards the first child. Legal advice should be sought and if disclosure is contemplated, every effort made to discuss the matter and to obtain consent.

Where a child is felt to be at risk of abuse, 'Working Together'[5] constitutes recognised good practice to be followed by the social and health services and the police. It recommends that information about children at risk should be shared between professionals and that the child's views should be made known at a case conference, usually through a social worker. Such advice is in potential conflict with many typical local authority policies on HIV and confidentialiy. In the case of an older child it is also in potential conflict with his or her right, following the decision in Gillick, to seek independent advice and counselling in confidence. The conflict can be readily reconciled in relation to HIV status if the child or parent consents to disclosure. Where disclosure is unavoidable for child protection reasons the Local Authority Association's working group recommends that consent should still be sought and if withheld, the fullest explanation must be given as to any disclosure made.

Adoption

The adoption of children is another area of potential difficulty. The procedure is governed by the Adoption Agencies Regulations 1983 (Adoption Agencies Regulations [NI] 1989). Under these regulations the adoption panel's medical adviser must obtain a full health history of the birth parents, up-to-date medical reports on the prospective adopters and prepare a full report on the child's health, arranging such examinations and screenings as considered necessary. The reports on the child and the prospective adopters are expected to be very detailed and to include any relevant information which may assist the adoption panel in reaching a decision, including in the case of adoptive parents, details of their daily consumption of alcohol, tobacco and any habit-forming drugs.

If a placement is approved, it is the medical adviser's responsibility to provide the prospective adopters and their family doctor with information on the child's health and to notify the local education authority and district health authority (Education & Library Board in Northern Ireland) of the placement. It would, in my opinion, be impossible to argue that the adoption panel and prospective adopters should not be given all existing information about the child's HIV status and any known risk factors. According to the DES guidance,[6] it may not be necessary to disclose the child's HIV status to the local education authority.

All adoption records, including medical reports, are to be kept by an adoption agency in a place of special security for 75 years and are treated as strictly confidential subject to disclosure by the medical adviser as described above and various other exceptions. Local authority adoption records are at present exempt from disclosure under the Data Protection Act 1984.

Routine screening of children who are to be placed for adoption is sometimes proposed. This is a matter for each individual authority to decide, subject to the general comments on consent to and confidentiality regarding the testing of children set out earlier in this chapter. It is not at present recommended by BAAF, and in most areas calls for routine testing are discouraged, other than in cases where there is a clear risk, with potential adopters being told that it is not possible to guarantee that a child is free of HIV infection.

Care and accommodation

A local authority has numerous statutory duties towards children in its area who are subject to care orders or who are being 'accommodated' by the local authority. Both categories of children are now described as 'looked after' by the authority. The grounds for making a care order, whether in the magistrates' court, county court or High Court have been standardised and are as follows:

a) that the child concerned is suffering or is likely to suffer significant harm and,
b) that the harm, or likelihood of harm is attributable to:
  i) the care given to the child, or likely to be given to him if the order were not made, not being what it would be reasonable to expect a parent to give to him; or
  ii) the child's being beyond parental control. (S.31, Children Act).

Additionally, the court is required to give paramount consideration to the child's welfare in accordance with a check list of relevant factors listed in section 1(3), and in each case may only make an order if it considers that to do so is better than making no order at all. An order may not be made in respect of a child who has reached the age of 17 and cannot continue beyond the child's 18th birthday. The new grounds allow for the making of care orders in two particular situations not adequately covered by the old legislation: firstly, in respect of a newborn child or other child who is considered to be at risk but who has not yet been harmed and secondly, where a child is being accommodated and the local authority objects to his or her return home and can establish grounds for this. If an order is made, the local authority must provide for the child's accommodation and maintenance, and it acquires parental responsibility for the child.

The fact that a child has HIV infection does not of itself constitute grounds for a care order. However, a care order may be made in respect of children with HIV infection in other circumstances, for example, those whose parents' drug abuse is placing them at risk, or who are being sexually abused. In the case of very small children and babies their own HIV status may be uncertain.

Accommodation may also be provided for any child who is in need and who requires it because there is no one with parental responsibility, he or she is lost or abandoned, or the usual carer is unable to care for or accommodate the child (S.20). The local authority does not acquire parental responsibility and the child may be removed at any time by a person with parental responsibility.

A child in need is defined as one who is unlikely to achieve or maintain a reasonable standard of health or development, or whose health or development are likely to be significantly impaired without the provision of local authority services, or who is disabled (S.17(10)). The definition of disability is likely to encompass a child with AIDS, and children whose parents have HIV or AIDS may also be 'in need'. Children whose parents are unable to care for them by reason of their own ill health may be accommodated under these provisions.

A young person of 16 or over may request accommodation in his or her own right which should be provided if the authority considers that his or her welfare is otherwise likely to be severely prejudiced (S.20(3)).

positive pupils. These incidents were resolved through public education via meetings and without recourse to the courts. A similar approach was taken more recently when in April 1991, controversy arose in Kirklees over the presence of a child with the Hepatitis B virus in a state school. By way of contrast, there is now a string of cases in the USA, some brought on behalf of HIV positive children, seeking to enforce their right to attend school, and others brought by other parents trying to exclude them. Successful claims for inclusion at school have relied on federal law prohibiting discrimination against the disabled in any programme receiving public funds (eg *School Board of Nassau County* v *Arlene*). The UK does not have a similar law. Other successful claims have been brought under legislation guaranteeing disabled children's educational rights, for example, *White* v *Western School Corporation* where a boy was allowed back to school on receipt of a health certificate saying that he was not a danger to public health. In many of the US cases, pressure from other parents has led to the child's exclusion, and they have only been reinstated after legal action.

Special education

Special education provision is relevant to HIV in several ways: children who have AIDS may have special educational needs, other disabled children may be at risk of HIV infection (for example, through sexual abuse), and children who are HIV positive at birth may develop neurological problems and learning difficulties. DES advice on such children is that developmental delay and disability, together with HIV antibody status, will be taken into account in any assessment of the child's special educational needs. This involves a lengthy and cumbersome procedure colloquially known as 'statementing' which should result in the issue of a statement of Special Educational Needs under the 1981 Education Act (Education & Libraries [NI] Order 1986). Appropriate education should then be offered. This assessment can now be combined with any undertaken under the Children Act or other legislation to avoid multiple assessments.

Sex education and learning about HIV and AIDS

If we believe in the importance of good public health education to reduce the rate of HIV transmission, it is necessary to consider whether and how the subject is dealt with at school. Sex education lessons are an obvious forum for such teaching. These are regulated by the Education (No 2) Act 1986. This gives school governers the responsibility for deciding whether and in what form sex education should be provided. A survey published in June 1992[10] found that only 46 per cent of local education authorities in England and Wales had information regarding the sex education policies within schools in their area. Of these, 69 per cent of schools had a policy, 25 per cent had no policy and six per cent had adopted a policy against including sex education. It is essential under the law that the governors approve the proposed syllabus, which must ensure that sex education 'is given in such a manner as to encourage people to have due regard to moral considerations and the value of family life', and that parents should be consulted.

The Schools Inspectorate has given this advice:

'Teaching about the physical aspects of sexual behaviour should be set within a clear moral framework. Pupils should be encouraged to consider the importance of self-restraint, dignity and respect for themselves and others and helped to recognise the physical, emotional and moral risks of casual and promiscuous sexual behaviour. Schools should foster a recognition that both sexes should behave responsibly in sexual matters. Pupils should be helped to appreciate the benefits of stable, married and family life and the responsibility of parenthood.'

The Schools Inspectorate also recommends that teaching about homosexuality should not be avoided. It must take place within the ambit of Section 28 of the Local Government Act 1988 which provides that a local authority must not 'intentionally promote homosexuality nor promote the teaching in any maintained school of the acceptablilty of homosexuality as a pretended family relationship.' With HIV no doubt in mind the statute goes on to provide that it should not 'be taken to prohibit the doing of anything for the purpose of treating or preventing the spread of disease.' Parents are allowed to withdraw their children from sex education lessons.

Education about HIV was introduced into the National Curriculum as part of the science syllabus in September 1992. This may be a way of ensuring that, notwithstanding the views of the governors, children are educated on HIV in a subject area which is outside their control, and as such, has already elicited controversy.

References

Index of cases

- Re E, The Times 22.2.91; January (1992) Family Law 15
- Re J (a minor), The Times 15.7.92
- Gillick v West Norfolk and Wisbech Area Health Authority, (1985) 3 All England Law Reports 402; (1986) IFLR 224
- Re R (a minor) (1991) 3WLR 592; NL3 27.9.91
- A v Liverpool City Council (1982) AC 363; (1981) 2FLR 222
- Re B (a minor), 2 FLR 426 1991
- Re C (a minor), Family Law 524 December 1991
- W v Edgell, All England Law Reports, 835, 1990

Further discussion of the US cases quoted may be found in AIDS Law published by the AIDS Legal Referral Panel, San Francisco Bay Area 1990

Regulation and Circulars

1 *The Children Act 1989 Guidance and Regulations* Volumes 1-8, HMSO, 1991
   See also *Children and HIV: guidance for local authorities*, a document issued by the Department of Health for consultation after the preparation of this chapter.

2 *Professional conduct and discipline: fitness to practice*, General Medical Council, 1992.

3 *HIV infection and confidentiality*, The Local Authority Association's Officer Working Group on AIDS, 1989

4 *HIV and AIDS: A guide for the education service*, DES, 1991

5 Home Office/DOH/DES, *Working together*, 1991

6 See 4

7 *The Children Act 1989 Guidance and Regulations*, Volume 3, Family Placements, Chapter 9, HMSO, 1991.

8 *The Children Act 1989 Guidance and Regulations*, Volume 4, Residential Care, Chapter 7, HMSO, 1991.

9 See 4

10 *An Enquiry into School Sex Education*, The Sex Education Forum, June 1992

5 Caring for children and families infected and affected by HIV/AIDS:
A social work perspective

Gerry O'Hara

Gerry O'Hara is Principal Officer, Children and Young People, at Lothian Department of Social Work. He has been concerned with work for families affected by HIV in Edinburgh since the infection was identified in the mid-1980s.

In Scotland 51 per cent of HIV positive reports are associated with injecting drug use with 60 per cent of these reports originating from Edinburgh. In Edinburgh it is estimated that one in a hundred men aged between 15–44 years and one in 250 women of child-bearing age are infected with the virus.

As Dr Mok reports in Chapter 3, evidence of HIV infection in pregnant women in Edinburgh has so far been found almost exclusively in women who have been intravenous drug users or whose partner is known to be HIV positive due to intravenous drug use. These women, who tend to live in areas of the city affected by multiple deprivation, may have many of the following characteristics:

– serious long-standing drug dependency problems;
– a history of offences – they may have been or currently are in prison;
– turbulent family backgrounds and relationships involving violence, alcohol dependency and a range of other problems;
– very little useful extended family support – other family members or partners may also be drug users and HIV positive and some of these women have themselves been abused as children;
– unwillingness or inability to use help all that easily from statutory agencies including social work – there is often a history of suspicion and mistrust;
– a tendency to deny the extent of their problems and the effect on their children;
– a likelihood that their children have previously been in care with or

sometimes without their consent;

– a pre-occupation with a whole range of social, emotional, economic and health problems;

– frequently being described as immature and unpredictable;

– often having partners in transient relationships fraught with violence.

Voluntary and statutory agencies will be familiar with working with families often labelled or described in this way, and will appreciate the enormous challenge in offering services designed both to support and sustain the families whilst at the same time meeting the needs of children who may require protection.

HIV infection in children

The discovery of HIV infection in Edinburgh in October 1985, with follow-up studies in 1986, indicated that the problem had probably been around since 1983. In particular, young people who had been injecting drugs were seen to be at risk and in a 1986 study at least 68 per cent of one cohort of drug users was known to be HIV infected. The fact that this group was almost exclusively heterosexual and 30 per cent female had very important implications for the spread of HIV infection in Edinburgh. Women, many of whom were of child-bearing age, were at risk because their sexual partners were injecting drugs, or they may have been doing so themselves. Children were and are at risk because of vertical transmission during pregnancy from mother to child.

The European Collaborative Study, which suggests a transmission rate of approximately 13 per cent, does not, of course, reflect the reality that all children born to HIV positive mothers are affected if not infected. Services offered by Lothian Regional Council Department of Social Work deal with children and families affected by HIV and do not draw particular distinctions between children affected or infected for the purposes of care, support and protection.

What services are required?

Edinburgh is perhaps in a unique situation in Europe for some of the following reasons:

– Drug use is apparent in various parts of the city almost in an environmental enclave and it is certainly a familial problem, that is, it

involves the whole family;
- Children born at risk of HIV infection may have older brothers or sisters and the impact on these siblings will be considerable;
- For children and families affected by HIV/AIDS the impact of bereavement will be profound;
- There is a high degree of uncertainty for children born at risk of HIV infection. For instance, the European Collaborative Study suggests that approximately one third of HIV infected children will develop AIDS, severe symptoms related to HIV or will die within the first year of life. The remaining two thirds of children will survive beyond the second year, and will follow a milder course or may even become asymptomatic in early childhood (see Chapter 3).

Families will require help and support in some or any of the following circumstances:
- Where the parent or parents are well and the children are well;
- Where the parent or parents are well and the child or children are ill;
- Where the parent or parents are ill and the child or children are well;
- Where both parties are ill.

In Lothian, services have been offered to families in all of the above categories. The following services, by no means exhaustive, are available for children and families where HIV or AIDS is an issue.
- Family support in the community, including counselling, practical help such as home care, occupational therapy, advocacy and liaison with other agencies;
- Supported accommodation to keep families together and provide extra support for single parents;
- Hospice care for the whole family;
- Day care, respite care, babysitting;
- Family Centre provision for children and parents;
- Foster or residential care;
- Adoption.

Principles underpinning the services for children and families at risk of HIV infection and AIDS
- The child's needs must have priority when deciding on the most suitable services;

- Every effort must be made to help birth parents to care for their own children in their own homes;
- Wherever possible, normal services available to other families should be used;
- Confidentiality on behalf of both parent and child must be maintained wherever possible;
- Carers, staff or substitute families, given good preparation and support, are well able to make decisions about their willingness to be involved;
- Stress resulting from caring for children at risk of infection, or who have become ill, means that carers will require extra support and back-up in the long run;
- Practices and policies must be reviewed regularly in the light of changing information and experience;
- There will be a need for individual case decisions in relation to some of the most sensitive issues, for example, testing children or telling particular carers about the HIV status of children in their care.

Increasing significance of HIV infection

Until 1989 it could have been said that the HIV status of parents was not the prime reason for services offered, or the reception into care of children affected. Families faced a myriad of social, emotional and economic problems which have required either short or long-term care for children. Since then, services offered, including reception into care, are increasingly required because of the HIV status of parents. Parents have become ill or have been hospitalised and have asked for help.

Flexible family and child-centred care

The remainder of this chapter concentrates on the need for, and the challenge of delivering flexible care to children and families in a variety of different circumstances. The recruitment, selection, training and support of carers is examined, including those issues concerning confidentiality, testing, and multi-agency and multi-disciplinary collaboration.

Flexible care must involve a range of services designed to support, sustain and care for children and families in adverse circumstances for as long as possible. Within this range of flexible support, Lothian has developed its foster care service so that families are able to use experienced carers offering friendship, babysitting, respite care and day care as well as longer term care as parents become ill and/or are less able to cope with their children. These carers will also be involved, as necessary, in providing for children whose parents die, offering a bridge towards a permanent new family, which sometimes may be found within the child's wider extended family. Inevitably some carers will offer permanent care to children who already will have become a part of their lives. However, it is important not to build that in as an expectation; rather, such a commitment should evolve as relationships develop.

These carers, who invariably in the past were more traditional foster carers, see their task as enabling children and families affected by HIV to remain together for as long as possible. They are, quite literally, on the frontline. They are required to respond to the needs of parents who may not have a history of 'good enough care' in relation to their children and whose developing illness will add to their unpredictable parenting, as well as to their erratic use of help.

Case study

Jill is 27, a single parent with two young children aged eight and six. She has full-blown AIDS and is frequently in hospital. She has no contact with her extended family other than occasional telephone calls. She has a range of health and welfare services, at the heart of which is her relationship with an experienced foster family who look after the children and, at times, Jill herself. As far as possible the care of the children is on an 'out of care' basis. In other words, they are rarely received into care. This is an important prerequisite for Jill. She was herself in care frequently as a child and has a terror of being separated from her own children, unless she can feel that she is still in control. So an agreement has been made that only if Jill is unable to make decisions regarding her children would they be received into care. Although up until now Jill has been neurologically fit, if, for example, she were to become demented she might not be able to exercise her responsibilities as a parent and therefore the children would be received into care.

The challenges for the foster family are many. They have to cope with a young woman who is frequently depressed, angry, abusive and resentful. At times she telephones and demands that the children be looked after or collected from school or picked up in the middle of the night because she has decided to go into hospital. She refuses to discuss her health and will not allow the carers to talk to her children about the possibility of her dying. She is not prepared, yet, to acknowledge that she will die, or will not be able to bring up her children and is most certainly not able to plan for their future. However, the carers believe that Jill's expectation is that they will look after the children.

The challenges for this agency and the carers involve taking risks. Jill frequently switches off as a parent. The children fend for themselves very often, and more than once Jill has left them alone in the house, although she always, eventually, phones the carers to collect them. The carers require much support. They know that they are on the frontline and are frequently having to make judgements about whether the children are being significantly harmed. The care team, which includes social workers for the family as well as for the carers, address these issues on a fortnightly basis and twenty four hour back-up support is available through the emergency duty service. However, the foster carers know that the delicate relationship between themselves and Jill could at any time be undermined to the detriment of the children. They want to care for the children and to help them prepare for their mother's death, whilst having some understanding of her current situation. They are frequently torn between their resentment of Jill and the way she treats both the children and themselves and their compassion for a young woman who has had very little life and who will soon die without seeing her children grow up. They are not sure whether they will be able to care for the children permanently although they are very attached to them, but certainly they have committed themselves to seeing the children safely and securely settled after their mother dies, whenever that may be.

Recruitment, selection, training and support of carers

As the example given illustrates, carers need to be experienced, well trained and supported. Lothian has recruited self-selected carers from the existing pool of experienced foster carers. All carers including day, respite, foster carers and prospective adoptive parents in Lothian are given regular information and training about HIV and AIDS. Those who wish to become more involved in this area are encouraged to decide for themselves whether or not they want further information and training with a view to becoming more specialised carers. Although there are a relatively small number of families positively committed to caring in different ways for children and families affected or infected by HIV, all foster families in Lothian are required to understand and accept that any child placed with them may well be infected. If they are not able to accept this then they will not be able to continue caring in Lothian. The reality is that we rarely know whether a child is HIV positive.

Caring families involved in this field share many of the following characteristics:

– mature people who have already had children of their own and have had good rewarding child care experience;
– experienced carers who have been used to caring for children with special needs and to working with parents;
– relatively non-judgmental and well able to maintain contact with parents even in difficult situations such as when they are in prison;
– seen to be 'family and child centred' with few if any worries about transmission of the virus to themselves or their family;
– having a well developed understanding of HIV/AIDS and very keen to keep up to date with information about their conditions.

Uncertainty about the status of the child and what might happen in the future is considered to be the biggest worry for carers. They say that the child's HIV status is always present but not dwelt upon, and that they alternate between optimism and pessimism in relation to the child's future and the future of the parents. In addition to support from individual link social workers, carers have the opportunity to attend a special support group of peers who are also involved in caring for infected or affected children. Additionally, direct medical support from an expert paediatrician and opportunities for respite are freely available. All of these services should, of course, be available to all families caring for children with special needs.

Testing

Testing for HIV infection is complicated medically. It poses many moral dilemmas because there is at present no cure for individuals who develop full-blown AIDS. However, as Dr Mok describes in Chapter 3, there is an argument for early diagnosis in order to initiate treatment which may delay the onset of full-blown AIDS. Agencies with statutory responsibilities must have as their principal aim the promotion of the welfare of the child. They require as much relevant information as is possible and available prior to placement in either a foster home or in an adoptive home. A selective approach is used aiming to identify children from backgrounds exposing them to the risk of infection, both when children are received into care and when adoption placements are made. This selective approach involves case by case consideration when children are referred for placement, and the following questions will be asked:

– Is there reason to believe that the child may be infected with HIV?
– Has this been discussed with the parent/s?
– Why should we know?
– How far should the question of whether the child is infected or not be pursued?

In all cases dealt with so far parents have been co-operative. If parents themselves are infected and the child was born after 1983, it is assumed that the child is at risk of infection and is placed accordingly. There would never be an attempt to test children without the permission of parents and the only justification for testing would be that for medical reasons, it was in the best interests of the child. If there is information to suggest that parents have been injecting drugs but are not aware or not willing to disclose their HIV status, the child would be placed and information given to the carers about the known background. There would be no attempt to push the family into giving information they did not wish to divulge or to go behind the backs of parents and approach the GP or hospital. Rather, an approach which seeks co-operation from parents is always followed; parents do wish to do what is in the best interests of their child.

Women seeking to place their babies for adoption are similarly treated and even if it is suspected that the child is at risk of infection, testing would not occur without the approval of parents after full pre-test counselling. If the social work department considers the child to be at risk and the parent does not wish to pursue testing, then the child would be placed and full information given to the prospective adopters. They, of course, would be able to have the child tested after the granting of the adoption order, but the department would not consider testing the child after the mother had given the child up for adoption and prior to the granting of the adoption order as this would amount to testing of the mother.

The only other circumstances in which testing would be considered would be if the child was unwell and HIV infection was suspected. In such cases, it could be argued that it would be in the best interests of the child medically to have a proper diagnosis with a view to early treatment with the range of therapies currently available.

Confidentiality

Lothian has developed its policy in relation to confidentiality in adoption, fostering, day and respite care placements on the basis of the following principles:

– There is no standard response to cover all circumstances;
– A distinction has to be made between disclosure of HIV status to colleagues, other carers, other clients and their relatives;
– The legal situation does not require disclosure of HIV or AIDS as this is not a notifiable disease;
– All carers require to be advised of the risk that any child placed with them might be affected with HIV;
– Clients or parents of children should be advised beforehand of the intention to disclose any information to carers even if this results in their refusing services offered by the department.

In summary, if the department knows that a child is infected with HIV, carers will be told. This is an interpretation of the legislation (both the Adoption Agency Regulations and the Fostering Regulations) but is also seen as a positive step in promoting the welfare of the child. The full-time care of children requires carers to know as much as is possible about children in order to ensure that they are looked after in relation to all their needs. The promotion of good standards of hygiene and the quality of care are seen as a fundamental part of preparation, training and support of all carers.

Beyond the immediate carers, the only other individuals who will be told about the status of children are the GP and health visitor. Anyone else can only be told with the agreement of the department and the parents, if appropriate and after careful preparation. This may, for example, be a relative who is seen as an important support person for the carer. Within families, carers are asked to judge for themselves, with help, whether or not their own children should be told, depending on their age and level of maturity and ability to hold the confidence.

Schools, nurseries and playgroups
It is the policy of this authority that neither teachers in schools nor nurseries nor leaders of playgroups need to have information about the HIV status of children placed with them. If teachers or play leaders were told it would be for very good reasons in individual cases. Usually, this is a parental decision and is often because of anxiety about protecting the infected child, rather than to alert other children and parents. As children become more ill, decisions have to be reviewed and evaluated in the light of the reality of the day to day care, but are always linked back to basic principles as stated above. Training, advice and guidance on HIV infection have been made available to schools, nurseries and playgroups.

Multi-disciplinary collaboration
Health care workers and others have had to learn to work together in dealing with this epidemic. Although at practitioner level in Lothian there were good relationships in the child care/child health arena prior to 1983, much closer collaboration has been required since then. It has been suggested that doctors have had to 'discover counselling' in the absence of a cure. This cynical view says much about the changes practitioners in both health and social work have had to make to understand the whole needs of children and adults infected and affected by HIV and AIDS. It is not exclusively a health issue nor is it merely a welfare challenge. Trust, understanding and mutual respect need to be achieved if services are to be coherent and used by the families who need them. Training, education, care and treatment are multi-disciplinary challenges. The

lessons of HIV in Lothian include the necessity of a holistic approach with each worker/professional being clear about the boundaries, responsibilities and potential of their role.

Voluntary agencies in the drug field are having to address the issues of child protection in the context of a traditionally adult centred service. Both statutory and voluntary agencies require to understand each others' roles and responsibilities within a climate that recognises the relative strengths of the agencies. In other words, if voluntary agencies, particularly in the drug field, are more successful in working with families, the statutory agency should harness this strength, financially and in other ways. Voluntary agencies need to take responsibility for ensuring that any help they give is underpinned by the need to protect children in situations where they may be neglected, abandoned or abused. Working with children and families infected or affected by HIV and AIDS is one of the great challenges of multi-agency collaboration.

The future

As the epidemic unfolds, specific needs are becoming clearer. In Lothian, demands for services to children and families are changing significantly as adults become more ill and are dying. Support for children and parents is vital. And flexible care and carers are essential.

6 **Working to a deadline:**
Planning for children affected by AIDS

Carol Lindsay Smith

Carol Lindsay Smith is Development Officer for HIV/AIDS services at Barnardo's. She was formerly Project Leader at Barnardo's New Families, first in Glasgow and then in Colchester.

Anticipating that some parents who have HIV infection will need help to make secure plans for their children whom they may not see through to maturity and independence, Barnardo's has developed a self-referral planning scheme: Positive Options is based in central London but available to parents in any part of the country. The background to the scheme is described below; the scheme itself is outlined at the end of this article.

One of the side effects of AIDS is the number of children who will need intermittent or permanent care when their parents become too ill to carry on. In most families the first choice would be care by relatives or friends, but this will not always be achievable. In such cases, social workers will be called in to find a solution, working, as usual, with too few resources and harsh time limits on behalf of distressed children who themselves may be terminally ill.

At the present time most homefinding agencies in the UK have had little experience of planning for children who have HIV or AIDS or who are indirectly affected through the illness of their parents. Staff are conscious of not being ready but, at the same time, have found it difficult to adapt work practices and prepare families in a vacuum; some level of expectation also persists that this difficult work will be performed only by AIDS experts. So, despite the long drawn out nature of the illness which should make it possible to prepare the child and have a family waiting, there have been examples of last minute arrangements, with children's fears and sadness over the loss of parents compounded by uncertainty about their own future.

While not wanting to underestimate the complexity and emotional content of working with AIDS, this contribution is written with the hope of reassuring agency staff and potential carers that the good practice skills, experience and systems which they already possess are valid for working with families touched by AIDS. With the addition of a basic level of AIDS awareness amongst staff and carers and resourcefulness in tapping into local AIDS units, it should be possible to provide a competent, discreet and safe service wherever the need arises. The Children Act 1989 is a bonus in that its main principles support a style of work well suited to working constructively with families facing AIDS.

The children needing family placement services

Up to now much concern has been focussed on the relatively small number of babies born to HIV+ mothers who may (but more likely will not) be infected with the virus. Many of these children will be cared for within their birth families. However, there will be some young children whose parents are too ill to cope or who will die first, leaving behind a child in poor health which may include neurological damage. In cases where there is no relative or friend to take over, adopters or foster carers will be needed who have the mental and physical stamina to care for a child whose health is declining and whose life span is likely to be short.

Far greater in terms of numbers and the span of years when care will be needed is the group of healthy children of all ages whose parents have the virus and who may not live long enough to see them through to independence. If no relative or friend is able to take over, these children will need supplementary parenting in the short term while their parents are ill but not yet ready to hand over responsibility, to be followed, in time, by permanent fostering or adoption when the parents can no longer cope or have died. The number of such children now, and in the future, is unpredictable.

Children from families affected by AIDS will have many of the characteristics and needs of other children needing substitute family care and potential carers will need all the usual qualities, training, experience and support. Additional factors for social workers and carers to take into account include the following:

– Some of the children will come from families who have had no practice at being 'clients' and who will not take kindly to having their lives talked about and organised by professionals who may have a different agenda and timescale to their own. Some of the children will have enjoyed relatively 'normal' lives until HIV intervened. They may not have the problems of deprivation and disturbance that carers are geared to handle, but instead will be bereaved, stigmatised, pining for their former life style, and with much closer ties to friends, places, pets and possessions. Such children will not join new families with the same sense of relief and excitement as children who have spent years moving around in care. One perceptive foster mother said: 'I know that even when she dies the mother will always be part of our family.'

– Parents who up to now have organised their own and their children's lives satisfactorily will resent their loss of independence – they may not be easy to help. On the contrary they may be competent, assertive, determined to stay involved to the last and sometimes unrealistically delaying on vital decisions. However inspiring it may be when the parent heroically refuses to admit defeat, it is devastating when that determination blocks all efforts to find a solution for the child. There is a great potential for conflict between the rights of the parent to carry on parenting and the needs of the child for security and relief from responsibility. In some cases commitment to partnership with parents will be tested to the limit.

– Other parents whose life style has brought them to the notice of the authorities in the past may fear to ask for help when they really need it in case their children are removed prematurely. Examples include a mother who refused hospital treatment for herself because she feared she would not retrieve her child from temporary care. Some parents with uncertain immigration status have foregone benefits and support for fear of identifying themselves; parents in these circumstances will need tactful outreach and confidence building to ensure their children get the services they need.

– The pattern of illness is so unpredictable that plans made when a parent seemed near to death may need to be reversed if the parent literally has a new lease of life. Potential carers will need the flexibility and the generosity of spirit to be demanded of, and dropped, by turns.

– Caring for a child who has HIV will bring the added stress of living with an unpredictable chronic illness and the likelihood of early death as well as doing so without being able to explain it all to friends and neighbours.

– In some cases carers may also find themselves parenting the parent who, on top of being ill, may be isolated from family and friends, using drugs, facing stigma and harassment, homeless, struggling with a foreign language and culture, or barely existing on benefits. For some families AIDS will be one of many complex problems.

Issues for mainstream adoption and fostering agencies

Given existing workloads and financial restrictions, it may be difficult for agencies in areas where there is as yet low incidence of HIV to justify major developments; there is also the problem of devising a system and preparing carers before having direct experience of what is needed. But there are some initial steps which will help them be prepared (and which may well apply to other client groups). These include:

– A simple written statement which explains what confidentiality actually means in this context, clarifies who needs to be told, what to record, how much detail to share with colleagues and in meetings. Families generally understand that information cannot stay with just one person but they need reassurance that it will not go all round the building and beyond.

– Advance planning about which members of staff need to be involved so that families are not swamped with well-intentioned extras: when several teams are involved (hospital, homefinding, child protection, home care...) this includes being clear about who takes the lead in meetings and who processes the plans. Since mention of AIDS has a tendency to paralyse common sense the need for clear strategies cannot be overstressed.

– Simultaneously working out how to maintain confidentiality without stifling essential discussion and homefinding advertising.

– Awareness that the HIV and AIDS factor can overshadow children's other basic needs. In this respect it is important for decision makers to have up-to-date knowledge of HIV and AIDS so that discussion is not disabled by fear of saying the wrong thing, and plans are not distorted by outmoded information (for example, that it would not be safe to place a child who is HIV+ into a family with other young children).

– Anticipation of the care needs of young children with the virus who may not have long to live by thinking creatively about who in the community could provide supplementary or longer term care; for example, should we be sending signals to grand-parents with a health care background who have the personal resources and energy to care for a child who is dying? Or is there a case for enlisting adults who are themselves HIV+ and currently healthy to provide short-term care and support to parents?

– Resolving in advance the financial and resource management implications of keeping a useful family on hold for a child who needs intermittent care when so many other children are also waiting.

– Before specific situations arise, preparing prospective adopters to have more involvement with birth parents and other relatives than has been traditional practice in adoption.

Positive Options

Barnardo's Positive Options Planning Scheme attempts to take account of some of these factors and to provide a straightforward, easily accessible service for parents who realise they need to make plans for their children but who have not felt able to turn to the statutory services. The aims of the scheme are:

– to encourage parents who have HIV infection to look ahead, to consider all the options (the first choice being care within the family or with friends) and, only when there is no other solution, to consider adoption or fostering;

– to involve parents at all stages of the plan, ideally achieving an open fostering or adoption while they are still well enough to be fully involved;

– to give high priority to the child's wishes in the context of what can be achieved that is both safe and lasting;

– to act as intermediary where necessary between parents and statutory agencies so that they make the best use of the full range of support and services;

– to make plans as early as possible and then get on with living and enjoying the time that remains.

Practical arrangements

The Planning Scheme is based in an informal office near the Angel, Islington, close to public transport.*

- Referrals may be by social workers or doctors or parents may come direct. Full name and personal details are not requested.
- The service is available by letter, phone or in person. Where travelling is a problem, efforts will be made to take the service to the family.
- Information is available on the full range of statutory and voluntary services including the legal and financial aspects of transferring the care of the child to others.
- Direct work is undertaken with children and young people in helping them understand the situation and involving them in making plans.
- The Planning Scheme is not an adoption agency but will refer parents to appropriate statutory or voluntary agencies.

In the following chapter, Joan Fratter describes the workings of the scheme.

---

*354 Goswell Road, London EC1V 7LQ, Telephone: 071 278 5039

7 Positive options planning scheme

Joan Fratter

Joan Fratter is a social worker in Barnardo's Positive Options Planning Scheme, responding to the needs of children and families affected by HIV. She was formerly Project Leader at Barnardo's Homefinding project at Barkingside.

The Positive Options Planning Scheme, a Barnardo's initiative, provides a straightforward and easily accessible service for parents with HIV infection who realise that they need to plan their children's future. The scheme encourages parents to plan ahead and to consider all possible options for the care of their children. The scheme involves parents at all stages of the plan and gives high priority to the wishes of the child. Parents can be referred through self-help groups, by social workers or doctors, or they can refer themselves.

Positive Options began to accept referrals from October 1991 and in the first six months, some 30 families had been in contact to discuss the future care of their children, having initially approached the Planning Scheme or Positively Women (a Positive Options children's worker is seconded to the latter).

Parents in contact with Positive Options

Most of the parents were referred by colleagues in statutory and voluntary agencies, including solicitors, doctors and nursing staff in Genito-Urinary Medicine Clinics, hospital-based HIV social workers, hospice counsellors, local authority social workers and counsellors in specialist HIV agencies such as BHAN (Black HIV and AIDS Network) and the Terrence Higgins Trust. Only a minority referred themselves. Most of the parents were women who were caring for their children without a partner; in some cases the children's father had already died and other relationships had not been strong enough to withstand the stresses imposed by HIV infection. However, there were a few two-parent families where both parents had HIV and one family was headed by a young man who was caring for his brother and sister. Some of the parents had no relatives living within easy reach; this was particularly true of those African parents who were refugees who had fled to the UK without relatives who would ordinarily have provided care for them and their children. Others had relatives living reasonably close by but had isolated themselves for fear of rejection if they disclosed their HIV status.

The parents came from a range of ethnic and cultural backgrounds. With one exception, they were all from well-functioning families who would not have needed support from statutory and voluntary agencies had it not been for one or both parents being infected with HIV. (This is a very different picture from Lothian where the majority of parents have become infected through drug abuse, and some of whom have been described as having chaotic lifestyles. See Chapters 3 and 5.) However, as more infected parents become unwell, some of them will no doubt include parents who have other problems in addition to HIV.

The number of children in the families ranged from one to four. Almost all the children were presumed uninfected, having been born before their mother contracted HIV or, if born subsequently, having tested as negative. However, in three families there was a child infected with HIV, and of these, two had brothers or sisters who were not infected, and one child was too young to be tested.

The parents had approached the Planning Scheme at different stages in terms of their HIV infection: a few were asymptomatic but most had one or more AIDS-related conditions or had not yet been diagnosed as having AIDS but were in need of periods of rest and hospital care and at times feeling unwell and fatigued. A few had been unaware of their HIV infection until they had been admitted to hospital and had then been diagnosed as having an AIDS-related condition. These parents had had very little time to adjust to being HIV positive at the stage at which they had approached the Planning Scheme. Others were wanting to resolve issues regarding their children's future care yet hoping that they themselves would be well enough to provide care for a few more years.

Although the Planning Scheme is available to families anywhere in the UK, all the referrals received in the first six months were from London and the South East. At the time of referral, none of the parents was able to combine caring for children and working full-time in paid employment and most were managing on benefits. For many, the stress and problems resulting from their HIV status were compounded by poverty and, in a few cases, inadequate housing.

Most parents approaching the Planning Scheme were unsure what services could be offered with regard to their children's immediate and long-term care and a few were anxious about approaching a social services department for fear of losing their children. It has been important for parents to know that Positive Options offers an independent and confidential service. However, a statement prepared for parents does explain that as a child protection agency, Barnardo workers might need to pass on or act on information if a child's health or development is at risk. Such a situation has not arisen during the first six months.

Most parents had received good counselling and support from a range of statutory and voluntary agencies, although there were some exceptions. While many parents declared that on learning of an HIV or AIDS diagnosis their immediate concern was the future care of their children, the additional concerns surrounding their condition, compared with other life-threatening conditions, prevented their being able to focus on planning. Some felt a sense of guilt as well as loss about not being able to care for the child through to independence, and parents have also had to cope with uncertainty about how the disease will progress and how long they will be able to spend with their child. Many were in fear of others discovering their HIV status, particularly neighbours or members of their community. Their awareness of stigma, prejudice and hostility regarding AIDS has caused them to be anxious about what to tell their children and how. Additionally, for many the situation is exacerbated by the attitudes and expectations of society and the media: black families face racism and discrimination; women carers with HIV or AIDS often have difficulty in prioritising their own health needs; parents who are refugees are likely to feel exceptionally vulnerable; lesbian or gay parents have to contend with homophobia. Inevitably there are times when a parent's ill health, mental distress or emotional pain may make it difficult to work with them during a particular session in the way that had been planned.

Parents may have a clear idea about friends or relatives who could be guardians, adoptive parents or foster carers to their children in the longer term, but may need help in understanding the legal and financial issues, and sometimes, in approaching friends or relatives who may be unaware of their HIV status. Other parents may believe there is no-one to whom they can entrust the child's long-term care and may need advice and an intermediary in requesting foster care or adoption from the local authority. Most have needed help in understanding what services they are entitled to for their children to enable them to care for them as well as they would like to; all have needed to discuss when and how to prepare the child for their eventual death. Clearly there are additional considerations if one of the children also has HIV.

The Children Act
The Children Act 1989 has enormous potential for helping children infected and affected by HIV and a few local authorities have offered a range of imaginative and flexible services. Some local authorities have explicitly included children affected by HIV as 'children in need', thus acknowledging the duty to safeguard and promote their welfare. Some of the key principles of the Children Act – the requirement to work in partnership with parents, to take account of children's wishes and feelings and of their race, culture, religion and language – are particularly applicable to working with families with HIV. Parents generally welcome knowing that the Children Act promotes the care of children within the family network and the sustaining of contact.

The Children Act acknowledges the need for domiciliary, day care and respite care services for children with disabilities and for children in need. Respite care, needed when a parent is unwell, debilitated or receiving hospital treatment, may be offered by friends or relatives, through private or local authority foster care or by someone moving into the family home to care for the children. All these arrangements can be made flexibly through the provisions of the Children Act, with the local authority providing accommodation or a carer or financing care offered by relatives or friends. An option which many parents would prefer – that of someone caring for children in their own home – has seldom been available, unless the parents can identify a relative or friend to undertake this or can engage someone privately (perhaps with resources provided by the Independent Living Fund). Social services departments have considerable experience in providing respite care arrangements for families with a child with disabilities, and this is usually family-based. However, respite care for affected and infected children may need to be more flexible and responsive to emergencies, because of the unpredictable nature of HIV. In the London area there is generally a shortage of local foster and respite carers who are able to care for brothers and sisters together and come from a range of ethnic and cultural backgrounds. In a few instances, this has meant that a parent who is currently well, and wanting to plan ahead by arranging for her children to get to know a respite carer, may be told that no accommodation can be arranged until she is ill. It is understandable that a hard-pressed local authority may be able to respond only to emergencies, but this is deeply disappointing to parents who would like themselves and their children to have the opportunity of developing a relationship with prospective carers. (Some parents have had the experience of their children being admitted to short-term foster care while they were in hospital, when there had been no opportunity for an introduction.)

The children

The children whose parents have approached Positive Options have ranged in age from four months to 16 years. While almost all the parents have been aware of the need to provide some continuity for their children through planning, they have varied enormously in their views about what information children should be given and when. For example, one mother had begun to talk to her six-year-old son about the fact that she might die before him (this little boy had some idea of the permanence of death because his father and a younger sister had already died). On the other hand, a mother of three teenage children was uncertain about their knowing that she had a terminal illness, and had been told that she was likely to die very soon. Parents have found it helpful to discuss ways of preparing children for their death. The African families with whom I work seem to find this task less daunting than do other families and are generally more open in their attitude towards death.

People also have widely differing views as to whether a child should be told that the parent has HIV or AIDS. While some children of junior school age have this information, other parents are wary of a child under ten being informed of the diagnosis, in case he or she inappropriately passes on the information outside the family and attracts prejudice and ostracism. Realistically, all children and young people who are informed of the diagnosis need to be given an opportunity to discuss who it would be safe to tell. There can be a dilemma for a worker who believes that, for example, a particular 13-year-old is entitled to know of the HIV diagnosis although the parent forbids this information to be passed on. In one case, a mother had not told her teenage children of her diagnosis, although she had prepared them well for her death and they were fully involved in plans for the funeral and their future care. When the children learned of the diagnosis after their mother's death, they were upset and angry, not because their mother had had AIDS but because she had 'not trusted us enough to tell us'.

In common with any other children being separated from their birth parents, children affected by HIV will need a knowledge of their identity and their family history. Parents are encouraged to compile a family book for the child (this is modelled on the common practice of life story work for children in care). Parents who feel well enough have enjoyed participating in a video, which may include a parent talking about his or her own family background as well as scenes showing the children and parents together on a special occasion or outing which can be remembered in the future. A 'memory store' has been designed to incorporate not only a family book, a video and an audio tape, but also special mementos and treasures of particular significance. Where a child is eventually going to be living with a member of his or her birth family, a parent may not feel it is important to compile a family history but the making of a video is usually seen as very worthwhile. The amount of direct work to be undertaken with a child will vary, depending on the time available to the parent, his or her confidence in preparing the child and the possibility that another trusted adult, perhaps a buddy or volunteer from a voluntary agency offering support to people with HIV, can help the parent. Because it is intended that the Planning Scheme service will be time-limited, it makes sense in situations where a parent is likely to be caring for a child for several more years, that an adult who will be continuing to be involved is there for the child. The Planning Scheme service consists of helping the parents to make the plan and set it in motion satisfactorily. Continuing social work support by the Scheme is not included, so it makes sense for another supportive adult to be involved, in order to provide continuity over time for the child.

The needs of a child whose parents have HIV are very similar to those of any child facing loss and separation and can be summarised as follows:
– information appropriate to the child's age and understanding about the parent's condition;
– a trusted person to talk to;
– preparation for bereavement:
>   involvement, not exclusion
>   permission to have angry/sad feelings
>   not to feel blame
>   factual information about death/funerals
– not to become an unsupported young carer;
– appropriate consultation regarding future plans, including:
>   clarity regarding legal status (who will have parental responsibility?)
>   plan for contact in the future
>   regard for his/her race, religion, culture and language
>   knowing the parent approves the plan
– knowledge of identity and family history.

Planning care for the child

The diagram on the following page illustrates the options available to parents in the short and the longer term and how they may link together. With the exception of the adoption column, the forms of short-term and respite care may be different from the permanent care planned for the future.

The range of options can best be described through individual situations:

Maria is a 29-year-old black woman with sons aged nine and six and a daughter aged two. Maria is in relatively good health although she often feels tired. She receives a good level of emotional and practical support from voluntary agencies. Maria's main concerns are centred on the fact

Available options

	Relatives/Friends	Live in carer	Foster care	Adoption
Short/medium term support Respite Emergency	Entitled to receive financial or practical support from statutory or voluntary agencies	Privately arranged or provided by statutory or voluntary agencies	'Task centred' Flexible Providing continuity	Via local authority or voluntary agency — Introductory meetings and time together — Befriending whole family — Respite
Permanent care	May become informal long-term carers or acquire parental responsibility through adoption, guardianship or residence order or be approved as a foster carer	May be non-related or may be a friend or relative May receive no remuneration or be employed by the local authority or fee earning May be approved as a foster carer May acquire parental responsibility	Provided through local authority or voluntary agency	Continuity provided through eventual placement for adoption

that her daughter has AIDS and her sons will have to cope with the death of their sister and of their mother in due course. When Maria has needed a holiday with relatives or convalescence in a hospice, a friend has moved in to care for the three children. This has been financed by the local authority, using Section 17 of the Children Act. There are relatives living too far away to offer day-to-day support but who are committed to caring for the children when Maria is too ill to do so. I have discussed with Maria how she can make arrangements to nominate these relatives as testamentary guardians, if she wishes to do so, and I have explained to them the implications of their taking on parental responsibility after Maria's death. (The children's father has already died.) The prospective guardians do not anticipate needing financial support other than the guardian's allowance and child benefit. (If they did, it would be possible at this stage to explore with the local authority whether financial help could be offered through Section 17; whether as an alternative to guardianship the relatives could apply to become foster carers and thus receive boarding-out payments; or whether they could apply for a Residence Order and receive an allowance.)

Anna, a white woman aged 32, has a seven-year-old son who is not infected. She approached the Planning Scheme at a time when her health was beginning to deteriorate and she had worries about her son's short-term and longer term care. She eventually identified a family whose daughter attends school with her son and the local authority has agreed to approve this family as respite foster carers for periods of short-term and emergency care. In the longer term, Anna would like her son to live with her brother and sister-in-law who live in Italy; the only alternative would be a foster carer or adoptive parent recruited through the local authority. Anna has not yet nominated her brother as testamentary guardian, however, as she would like to know that he could receive some financial support and it seems that despite the emphasis in the Children Act on promoting care of children with relatives, financial support may not be so readily forthcoming to a relative living outside the UK. Legal advice has been sought on this.

Jane and Michael are a white couple aged 29 and 34 respectively who both have AIDS. Their two children are aged five and seven. The family is quite isolated socially, having no contact with relatives and very limited involvement within their neighbourhood. Jane and Michael receive services from a large number of voluntary and statutory agencies including the hospice home care team, a childminder, a volunteer babysitter, a hospital social worker, a community psychiatric nurse, a counsellor from a self-help organisation and a local authority social worker. This bewildering but necessary team of workers has enabled Jane and Michael to provide continuity of care for their children when one or other has needed hospice or hospital care. However, they were put in touch with the Planning Scheme when they felt the need to make plans for the care of their children in the event of having to be admitted to hospital together and for the longer term. It emerged through discussion that there are no relatives or friends to whom Jane and Michael felt that they could safely entrust their children. They decided the most suitable alternative for the children would be an adoptive family, and hoped that an adoptive family could be identified as soon as possible, so that they could meet them and the children could begin to spend weekends getting to know them, as well as staying there should an emergency arise. There was much to be gained from such an arrangement: the birth parents would be reassured about who would be caring for their children after their death; continuity for the children and support during and after their bereavement would be provided; and the adoptive parents would feel confident about having gained the approval of the birth parents. This request initially proved challenging to the local authority. Like most agencies, there are separate teams of workers to deal with respite care and adoption. However, a local authority subsequently agreed to undertake to recruit an appropriate family.

Sandra, a white woman in her early thirties, was already seriously ill with AIDS-related illnesses when she approached the Planning Scheme. At that stage she had not begun to prepare the children or discuss her condition with any relatives. During her frequent hospital admissions the children, aged 11, 13 and 14, usually stayed with neighbours but on one occasion had been accommodated with local authority foster carers living locally. What Sandra and the children desperately wanted was for the children to be able to stay on in their own home with a live-in carer after their mother's death. Their father had not been married to Sandra and had left the family home some seven years earlier; he had never applied for parental responsibility. In order to avoid leaving the children without someone with parental responsibility, Sandra decided to nominate her sister and brother-in-law as testamentary guardians. I had embarked on the task of recruiting a carer (who would have alternate weekends off when the children would be cared for by friends or relatives) and at the time of the mother's death she had identified the person she thought would be most suitable. In the event, however, an adult relative of the children offered to move into the household, initially for a few weeks but then permanently. A very creative local authority underpinned the arrangement financially by acting as trustee for the tenancy of the council house (which the children will inherit when they come of age) and by approving the relative as a foster carer and providing her with an income through enhanced allowances.

Implications for practice in adoption and foster care

The work with parents through the Positive Options scheme has highlighted the need for a flexible and individual response. For example, some parents are able to identify relatives to care for their children in the short and the longer term and may need minimal involvement from the social services department. While some parents may be anxious to name a friend or relative as a testamentary guardian through the making of a will, others, particularly African and Caribbean parents, may not feel the need for such formality, confident that they can rely on friends and relatives to offer permanent care without any written agreement. A few parents will be dependent through the provision of statutory services for the children's long-term as well as short-term care. Some parents have expressed strong views about their child's religious upbringing (including a parent who stressed that her children should have no such input).

At the time of writing, not all social services departments have a written policy regarding the placement with adoptive parents and foster carers of children infected and affected by HIV, but some are working hard to offer a sensitive service. There is increasing recognition of the urgent need for child care workers in local authorities to learn from colleagues working with HIV infected or affected people and vice versa. Our perception in Positive Options, working with a large number of local authorities, is that to date, only a minority of statutory and voluntary adoption and foster care agencies are developing preparation and training to ensure that all prospective carers have an awareness of HIV and AIDS. Some agencies have not acknowledged the need for this, perhaps having been misled by the false assumption that only communities with drug users or people from Africa will need a service for children affected and infected by HIV and AIDS.

However, there is well-documented information that an increasing proportion of women from all sections of the community are becoming infected with HIV and a significant proportion are already, or will become, parents. The challenge to local authorities is to recruit and prepare, in anticipation, carers from a range of cultural and ethnic backgrounds who can provide flexible respite care, permanent foster care and adoption. Open adoption, which allows for continuing contact with members of the birth family, is particularly appropriate where parents can be helped to make plans well in advance for a child who has no relatives or other significant people able to provide care. Adoptive parents and foster carers from approximately 25 families have contacted the Planning Scheme (which is not itself a placing agency) indicating that they would like to become involved in supporting a family affected by HIV.

It seems certain that the number of affected children will increase rapidly during the next few years. I am confident that, as has happened in the past with so-called 'hard to place' children, there are adoptive parents and foster carers available for children who cannot be cared for within their family network. However, agencies need to be aware of the need, provide adequate training and support for workers and make a commitment to recruit and prepare people from all sections of the community.

Turn of the Wheel

I am so afraid
Now that the race is on
I must dig deep to find my faith
and the strength to carry on

The sword held by a thread
so sharp above our heads
twizzles like a pendulum
whilst the wheel that spins for all
withholds the final call

A gambler such as I
prays his luck will never die
yet knows instinctively
as he contemplates the dance
that he can't truly deny
the fickleness of chance

I know that God is great
I must ask Him if He'll wait
and let me spin and spin
to procure
my finest win

Written in August 1992 by a Positive Options parent who has AIDS and who has said that having to plan for the future care of his children is the 'most painful' thing he has ever had to do.

8 Issues for black families affected by HIV infection and AIDS

Hong Tan

Hong Tan is Director of the Globe Centre for people affected by HIV/AIDS in the city and east London. A biochemist by training, he first developed an interest in HIV issues through being asked to befriend an individual person with AIDS. He is closely involved with BHAN (Black HIV/AIDS Network).

This chapter challenges the myths about HIV infection and black* communities, in particular the origins of the virus. It also highlights pertinent issues for work with black communities and considers ways forward for developing good practice.

Working with black children

Good practice is necessarily based on ensuring equality of opportunity; this includes equality of access to appropriate services as well as the development of anti-discriminatory policies in the provision of these services. Because good practice in such provision has been patchy, various lobbies have succeeded in having issues pertinent to black communities written into both Acts of Parliament and Department of Health guidance.

Two recent pieces of legislation require statutory and voluntary services to take into account and plan to meet the needs of black children and communities. For the first time in any British statute, the Children Act 1989 states:

'In considering the needs of the children particular regard should

---

* The term 'black' is used to describe minority ethnic communities which may be distinguished by virtue of their race or ethnicity or colour of their skin. This term is increasingly used by people of African, Caribbean and Asian origin.

be had to their religious persuasion, racial origin and cultural and linguistic background (Section 74(6))'.

It is important to state that although black communities are often described as having religious, cultural and linguistic features, these also exist in many white communities. Thus, appropriate policies and services for all multiracial, multicultural, multi-linguistic and religious communities must include black communities.

Secondly, the White Paper *Caring for people: community care in the next decade and beyond*,[1] which led to the NHS and Community Care Act 1990 and its ensuing guidance, calls on joint statutory and voluntary planning of services for black and minority ethnic groups:

'The government recognises that people from different backgrounds may have particular care needs and problems. Minority communities may have different concepts of community care and it is important that service providers are sensitive to these variations. Good community care will take account of the circumstances of minority communities and will be planned in consultation with them.' (Ethnic communities: paragraph 2.9)

On the basis of these alone, more proactive work in the development and provision of appropriate and high quality services to black communities is required. However, it must be stressed that black UK citizens have a right to appropriate services and these must be developed in response to need.

HIV/AIDS infection in black communities

Very limited information exists on the current incidence of HIV infection within black communities, but some data does exist for the prevalence of AIDS.

Up to December 1990, nine per cent of the total cases of AIDS in the UK (368 of a total 4,098 cases) were among people categorised as 'black, Asian/oriental or mixed origin' whilst the ethnic origin of a further nine per cent could not be determined.[2] This is a marked over-representation when compared to the fact that only 4.7% of the general population in the UK comprises black people.[3]

Of particular relevance for work with black children is the significantly higher prevalence due to heterosexual transmission (41 per cent of total) compared to 'non-black' heterosexual cases (three per cent of total 'non-black' cases). Black homosexual or bisexual men were of a similar number, but were only four per cent of the total homosexual/bisexual male cases. Black children were also a majority (58 per cent) of the children deemed to be 'at risk or with an infected parent'.

The numbers of black people infected outside the UK is also relevant. Recent data from anonymous antenatal testing in various inner London clinics revealed much higher than anticipated levels of HIV infection in political refugees from East and sub-Saharan African countries. The findings were used to predict a rate of HIV infection in women attendants of between one in 250 and one in 550 in some inner London clinics. This was an order of magnitude higher than data from outer London test sites.[4] It is important to note, however, that these are preliminary findings and interpretation must be cautious as the sample was small. Two key areas of work should be first, the need to address any attitudes and feelings which may lead to increased prejudice against black people and second, the need to promote issues of concern to black people with HIV/AIDS in order to surmount the barriers which prevent dealing with the impact of HIV.

At least 128 people with HIV infection and AIDS received the services of the Black HIV/AIDS Network (BHAN*) during the period April to November 1991. These figures were derived from casework in London only and may show an underestimate in the number of black people with

---

* The Black HIV/AIDS Network (BHAN) is a self-help group which supports African, African-Caribbean, Asian and South East Asian people who are living with or affected by HIV/AIDS. The organisation provides the following community care and home support services: counselling, support groups, home support and volunteers, befrienders for black people living with HIV infection, advice and information about services which are linguistically and culturally appropriate to black communities.

HIV infection and AIDS, indicating that there is an urgent need for better data, not only in the UK but throughout the EC.[5]

Myths about HIV and black communities

In considering appropriate services for black children infected and affected by HIV, it is important to challenge various myths, in particular the racist myths about the origins of the virus, as well as generic myths about working with black communities.

The myth of African origins of the virus

Early reports on HIV prevalence led many people to believe the equation:

'High prevalence (per quota of population) = origins of HIV = blame'

Clearly, high HIV prevalence occurs in many countries, including some from the African continent. This does not indicate that the latter is necessarily the source of the infection, nor that Africa should be held responsible for the subsequent worldwide epidemic.

The blaming of HIV on Africans was shown to be based on spurious data and unscientific techniques.[6,7] These early studies were conducted using an enzyme linked assay technique (ELISA) which had a high level of false positives; one study showed a 60 per cent incidence of HIV positivity from blood samples using ELISA, but when using the much more accurate immunological assay, showed an incidence of only three per cent, which, although still quite high, is very different from 60 per cent. Other studies, using a sample of fewer than 50 people, translated their HIV prevalence into indication of the national incidence. This would be totally unacceptable for UK studies.

The testing of frozen blood samples from various African countries has been used to attempt to establish that HIV has existed in Africa for over 20 years, 'spreading in certain regions of sub-Sahara since the 1960s'.[8] However, the process of freezing changes the shape and activities of many proteins and similar testing of frozen blood in the USA has shown a similarly high percentage of false positivity.

Despite being refuted by the original researchers responsible for these spurious findings, the figures continue to be quoted as viable, particularly by the media.

It is important to compare the approach to prevalence of HIV infection in certain East/sub-Saharan African countries with that in the USA, which continues to have the highest numbers of AIDS cases worldwide. However, despite the high incidence in the USA, it is rare to find theories about HIV originating in the USA, rather than in Africa.

The myth of first HIV transmission due to sexual exoticism and activities
Another result of the 'African origins' myth is the assumption that the main source of transmission is by high levels of unprotected sex and by the supposed frequency of sexual activity of many African peoples. This has been seen by some to indirectly support the stereotype of 'sexual exoticism', that is, the sexually potent black man and the fertile black woman which was projected in the 18th century during the slave trade.

It is quite clear that although sexual transmission *may* be a main route of transmission in certain African countries, there are few research studies to prove it and indeed the same may be the case in many other countries. However, other factors, for instance, the mass vaccination campaigns of the 1970s where needles were persistently reused, may contribute equally to the spread of HIV infection, but are rarely mentioned in discussion about the incidence of HIV infection in Africa.

Various other hypotheses have been proffered: for instance, people having sexual relations with the African green monkeys (which are in fact infected with a species-unique form of HIV), or infection resulting from humans eating infected monkeys (again impossible because of the different forms of the virus). Another theory suggests that the infection is spread by bites from infected mosquitoes; if this were true, it would result in a much higher rate of infection in sub-tropical and tropical regions, including the Australian and Asian continents.

The myth of Africa as one entity
References to the prevalence of HIV in various African countries are usually ascribed to Africa rather than to particular named countries. This is probably due to ignorance and is tantamount to stating that HIV transmission in Europe reveals an identical pattern regardless of specific countries and that any study about HIV in, for instance, UK blood can be extended to apply to all of the countries in Europe. This is clearly

untenable; indeed, differing rates and routes of transmission have been identified in France, Italy and the UK.[9] Why then is Africa subjected to such treatment?

The myth of heterosexual activity as the main source of transmission
During HIV awareness training, participants often state that the main source of transmission among black communities is heterosexual sex. Although this may appear to be the case, there are complex issues surrounding the categorisation of sexual activities of black people as there are for any community or population group. Anecdotal evidence from the National AIDS Helpline (Minority Lines)[10] shows that sexual stereotypes exist and these need to be addressed. For example, some men do have sex with other men without labelling themselves as gay or homosexual or considering the resulting effects on their relationships with women. It is also clear from the same data that an equal number of black gay and bisexual men have AIDS as those identified as heterosexual, and that some of these men also have dependants including children and other relatives.

Working with black communities: issues to be addressed

Diversity within black communities
Black communities have often been grouped together as one minority ethnic group and services have been developed and delivered accordingly. On the same basis one would assume that services for all white people should be the same and differences in attitudes, cultures and languages between various European peoples be of no consequence. This clearly does not happen. It is evident that there are many diverse communities within each ethnic group and these should be taken into account.

There is a demand by black communities for local and flexible services. However, historically services have often been developed to suit the initial and often most vocal clients. For instance, services for those with HIV infection in the US and the UK have often been developed in response to demands made by men. It is also often accepted that if few people request a service, there is no need for it – a reason sometimes given for little or no investment in developing appropriate services for black communities.

However, it is often the lack of accessible information about a particular service which results in a low demand. A study of Asian families with children with learning difficulties revealed that despite a high number of children needing local services, there was a lack of knowledge about their availability. Of 23 children who were incontinent, only six of their families were aware of the incontinence laundry scheme, whilst only ten knew about the respite care scheme.[11] The lack of service demand and take up may be due to the need for more flexible services. One of the families in the above study – parents in their 60s – wanted respite care but, when told that it was only available in one or two week blocks, turned it down as they only required it on occasional nights in order to attend family functions.

Services and policies need to be prioritised and integrated
Where services exist for black communities, the service providers and receivers may often be marginalised. This was highlighted by two reports from the North West Region Social Services Inspectorate (SSI) which noted that:

> 'Improving services for African-Caribbean and Asian people . . . was a professional concern for social services practitioners to learn about accommodating the clients and for black clients to fit into departments . . . Provision marginalised in this way has little chance of influencing major departmental issues.'[12]

Black staff within organisations are often assumed to be race relations officers in addition to generic workers. Also, needs are translated as 'more black carers', 'more ethnic meals' or 'more face to face workers at grassroot levels' rather than the equally important issues of power sharing and prioritisation. Services and policies for black communities need to be 'owned' by all within an organisation.

There is no shortage of qualified black staff
Another myth is that services are slow to develop due to the shortage of black staff. Again, the SSI noted that 'the evidence . . . is that there is

no shortage of ethnic minority applicants for social services jobs if they are sought.'[13] The issues to be addressed, then, are the development of appropriate and accessible recruitment and equal opportunities policies.

The need and place for specialist services

Integration of work with black communities should not exclude the need for specialist services. Within the sensitive issue of same race placements, a commonly-held belief is that 'same race families cannot be found'. This is highly relevant when foster carers are needed for children affected by AIDS. However, adequately prioritised and resourced schemes *have* demonstrated success in recruitment, as shown by a study of local authorities which have actively reached out to the local communities.[14] For example, a placement team of 25 social workers in the London Borough of Lambeth (population 245,000) drew 210 black foster carers, whilst a similar authority, Rochdale (population 206,000), employed only three people to find black foster carers and attracted only three. Innovative outreach to religious and community centres, advertising in the local and the black press as well as open evenings conducted in languages other than English were used to attract foster carers.

Generic services for black communities need to be improved

The generic context of black communities is often poor health and inadequate local service provision. An example of this was shown in the 1990 National Audit Office report on maternity services[15] where the perinatal mortality rate in Bradford (with its high black population) was compared to Huntingdon (with its low black population): the Bradford rate was nearly three times higher than that of Huntingdon (13.5:1000 compared to 5.1:1000 respectively).

Numerous factors which characterise black communities result from individual or institutional inequality. A Department of Education report stated that 'for some Asian children . . . being racially harassed is a way of life'.[16] Such prejudice and harassment may have led to associating black communities with certain 'problems' and thus creating stereotypes, for instance, that Asians have cultural and linguistic problems and that African-Caribbeans have behavioural problems. These myths should be challenged and dispelled.

Other issues, such as inequalities in economic status and housing, multiply the problems experienced by black people with and affected by HIV infection and AIDS.

The issues to be addressed

Planning for services should be proactively integrated and appropriate
Ratna Dutt of the Race Equality Unit stated in 1990 that:

> 'Residential, domiciliary and respite care have been inappropriate to the needs of the black communities . . . black consumers are under-represented as clients receiving the preventative and supportive elements of social services provision.'[17]

Bad practice can be avoided by involving clients in planning the appropriate services. Various models of good practice have been outlined which involve users of services in service development and monitoring of quality.[18] This requires engaging in a 'user involvement continuum' with appropriate information, consultation, participation or control by the users of the service. Effort should be made to ensure that information about available services and access to them is appropriately translated, targeted and communicated to various communities.[19] Local groups should be involved in translation and outreach programmes which should be integrated with other information targeted to black communities, for instance, with campaigns about sickle cell anaemia and thalassemia.

Training and support of staff and carers
All social services staff need to be trained in HIV prevention, HIV and black communities as well as anti-racism and equal opportunities.[20]

HIV awareness training often deals with attitudes towards sexuality, and the theory that the main route of transmission in Africa is unprotected heterosexual sex is often used to emphasise that HIV infection is not exclusively an issue for gay men. Yet the issues around anti-racist stereotypes are dealt with to a lesser degree. Equal time and energy should be spent on dispelling all these myths.

Workers, whether voluntary or otherwise, should have access to appropriate supervision and support in dealing with issues relating to black people with HIV infection and AIDS. Sensitive consideration should be given to finding workers of the same race and cultural background to care for clients; failure to do so can result in people being denied essential services, as illustrated in the following case study.

Case study

A Muslim family was referred to a generic HIV voluntary group. The volunteer visitor to the family was a white man who had not been briefed about them. During the initial meeting, the man found himself with the two daughters in a room by themselves. Since the family observed various orthodox customs that require that men not be left alone with women or young girls, the volunteer was told to leave the home and no further contact was made with the voluntary group.

Redefining models of acute and community care for black people infected with HIV

Many of the current models of care have been developed by white gay men who have done much pioneer work in this field. However, some redefinition is required with black communities in mind with differing, more flexible models of care to complement and broaden the range of existing provision.

It is also clear that the models of counselling and support devised by many HIV voluntary groups such as small group sharing, self-help, co-counselling and ten-step programmes will not necessarily be commensurate with community support for black communities.

Same race placement policies and planning for the child

Earlier mention has shown that same race placement policies can and do attract black foster carers. It is important to recruit, train and involve potential carers or adoptive parents as soon as possible in the planning of the child's care, as illustrated in the case cited below.

Case study

The sole parent of a six-year-old had died of AIDS. The nearest relative was in Uganda, and the parent had left strict instructions that he wanted the child to be brought up in a Muslim family. Lack of planning meant that there were no funeral instructions for the parent nor any appropriate foster carers recruited for the child. The case took two months to sort out with numerous telephone calls to find the child's relatives. A transracial placement would not have been in keeping with the parent's wishes nor necessarily provide appropriate understanding of the child's needs.

Appropriate, accessible materials and community development

There is an acknowledged dearth of well-presented and accurate information about HIV targeted to black communities. This needs to be urgently addressed, and particular care should be taken regarding translations. (An example of poor translation is 'oral sex' in an English language leaflet being translated as 'verbal sex'.)

Ownership of the issues around HIV will need to be facilitated through community development. There are numerous models of work around other health and social issues which affect black communities, for instance, sickle cell anaemia, albeit with far less social stigma attached to them.

Conclusion

Issues to be explored and researched in relation to black communities include accurate data on the impact of HIV infection and AIDS; a quality assurance survey of services for black communities within the health, local and voluntary services; drug use as well as mental health issues in black communities.

HIV infection and AIDS add additional stigma to black people who are already living with multiple forms of inequality in access to high quality services. In addressing the issues for black children infected with or affected by HIV, it is important to challenge both generic and HIV specific prejudices about black communities if appropriate services are to be developed.

References

1 Department of Health, *Caring for people: community care in the next decade and beyond*, HMSO, 1989.

2 *AIDS/HIV Quarterly Surveillance Data*, Public Health Laboratory Service AIDS Centre and Communicable Diseases (Scotland) Unit, December 1990.

3 OPCS, *Labour Force Surveys*, HMSO, 1985, 1987.

4 *Lancet* 337, 1614-5, June 1991.

5 Haour-Knipe M, Migrants and Travellers Group, *Assessing AIDS prevention. EC concerted action on assession of AIDS/HIV prevention strategies, Lausanne*, Institut Universitaire de Médecin Social et Preventive, Cah REch Doc UIMSP no 72, 1991.

6 Chirimuuta R & R, *AIDS, Africa and Racism*: Burton-on-Trent Press, 1987.

7 Sabatier R, *Blaming others: prejudice, race and worldwide AIDS*, Panos Institute, 1990.

8 Anderson R, Prospects for the UK. The AIDS epidemic in the UK: past trends and future projections, 24-30 in *HIV & AIDS, an assessment of current and future spread in the UK, proceedings of symposium, 24 November 1989*, 1990.

9 See 8 above.

10 Tomlinson K and Dade M, *Issues for clients and workers from black and ethnic minority communities: living and working with HIV*, discussion paper 3, CCETSW, 1989.

11 Cocking I and Athwal S, A case for special treatment, *Social Work Today*, 22, 12 February 1990.

12 Hughes R D, *Social services for ethnic minorities*, North West Region Social Services Inspectorate, 1986.

13 Hughes R D and Bhaduri G, *Race and culture in social services delivery*, North West Region Social Services Inspectorate, 1987.

14 Riddock F, 'Out of the background', *Social Work Today*, 22, 8 February 1990.

15 National Audit Office, *Report on Maternity Services*, HMSO, 1990.

16 DES, Swann report, *Education for all*, HMSO, 1985.

17 Dutt R ed, *Black community and community care*, Race Equality Unit, National Institute of Social Work, 1990.

18 *Quality and contracts in the personal social services,* Association of Metropolitan Authorities (AMA), 1991.

19 *HIV infection and the black communities*, Local Authority Associations' Officer Working Group on AIDS, AMA 5, Sources of help, 1990.

20 See 10 above.

9 Helping children and families to cope with bereavement

Juliet Swindells

Juliet Swindells is a social worker at the AIDS/Haemophilia Centre, Thanet District General Hospital, where she has developed strategies for preparing members of affected families to cope with bereavement.

The AIDS/Haemophilia Centre in Thanet cares for haemophiliacs and others infected with HIV or AIDS. In the course of our work we have to address the issue not only of children and teenagers who are HIV positive, but also the needs of children in a family where a parent or sibling or other close relative is infected with HIV. The cornerstone of our philosophy of caring for these children and families, evolved over the years, is to be as honest and as open as possible with the children, while respecting at all times the wishes of parents and families. We try to work alongside the families rather than impose decisions and solutions, respecting the individual needs each situation creates, and that what is right for one person may not necessarily be right for another.

Children and teenagers infected with HIV

An honest and open approach
Our belief in an honest and open approach to children stems from a wide field of experience which has demonstrated the high level of awareness most children have of what is going on in their family and immediate environment. Children, at quite an early age, pick up very subtle clues that all is not well, and if no explanation is forthcoming it is left to their imaginations to guess the exact nature of the problem. The imagination of the young is highly productive and inventive and can therefore produce some quite terrifying images to explain away the whispering behind closed doors or the walls of silence they encounter. Ignorance is very rarely bliss and most children usually deal far better with a truthful

explanation than with a scenario created by their wild imaginings.

Once diagnosed as HIV positive, all the evidence of infection becomes immediately apparent to them. This has been amply exemplified by our observations of haemophiliac boys attending our centre. They were suddenly having to attend hospital more frequently; doctors and nurses in attendance were wearing gloves and sometimes gowns and masks; if admitted to hospital the boys were isolated in side wards whereas they had previously been on the open ward. They perceived that something was wrong, something had changed. Being aware of their HIV infection actually reassured them of their ability to make sense of their world, their perceptions having been proven to be accurate.

Parental concerns
Having stated that it is best to be truthful, I do not want to underestimate the problems that many parents experience in arriving at a point of feeling able to cope with their children's awareness. To this end, we have set out to consider the emotions experienced when moving towards a more open awareness with their children, and to try to work through some of the confusing feelings they encounter.

In order to be able to cope with children's feelings we have first of all to cope with our own, to feel comfortable with ourselves. Some parents have talked to us about the guilt they feel at passing on the gene that causes haemophilia, or even allowing their children to have Factor 8 injections. It is very important to be able to talk about and come to terms with these feelings before beginning to relate to the needs of the child. Other parents have expressed fear about HIV because of the questions children might ask. Only one question gives cause for real alarm: 'Am I going to die?' Death is still the great taboo subject, even more so than sex. Perhaps this is not surprising in a society that lacks any spiritual philosophy about death, and where many people will still go to extraordinary lengths to avoid it. Does one handle the question of death any differently when discussing it with a child who is HIV positive or a child who is not? Surely the answer to 'Am I going to die?' is the same whatever the individual circumstances: 'Yes. Like everyone else you will die one day, but also like everybody else none of us know when.' One can then build in their particular religious or spiritual philosophy. This,

I know, is a very difficult area for many parents and again it is important to feel comfortable with one's own feelings about death before handling the issue with children.

There is also confusion about how much information you should give a child about HIV, and at what age to give it. Our philosophy in Thanet is quite simple: children are ready to know when they ask. The advice we give to parents is to be prepared to respond to any request for information, to keep the answers as simple as possible (there is always a great temptation to overburden children with information they have not asked for) and to create an environment where the child can always return to ask further questions in the future. It often helps parents to understand something or other about the emotional and psychological developmental stages that children go through, and how they perceive the world at different ages. Thus, while the parents' concerns, for example, for their ten-year-old who is HIV positive may include future abstractions about whether he or she will be able to marry, have children or buy a house, the child's horizons are far more limited. The child is concerned with the immediate future and environment, for example, would their HIV status prevent them from playing in a school team?

Another example of parental concern is the tendency to explain their child's behaviour solely in the context of their HIV status. HIV can become a useful peg on which to hang excuses for any manifestation of unruly or anti-social behaviour in their children. This can happen frequently during adolescence. The issue of sexual counselling must also be addressed during the teenage years. What do you say to the teenager who is HIV positive? Our experience in Thanet suggests that sexual counselling should not be centred around HIV. We ask our teenagers what sort of sexual relationship they would ideally like, and whether they prefer multiple relationships or prefer to restrict their sexual activity to more special relationships. Usually they opt for the special relationship as their ideal and within this context we then discuss the safe sexual practices they should adopt.

Our working practice aims to facilitate communication between parents and children. Once families begin to erect emotional barricades to avoid certain issues, repercussions spill out into other areas of their lives. Thus, in the consultation setting, we treat the family, not just the child. As far as possible we are honest and open with the children we care for. We never ever leave them sitting outside the door while we discuss medical and social implications for their future. When they visit for a medical appointment, the whole family is welcome to attend: mum, dad, siblings, grannies and any significant other who shares in the care and welfare of the child. When planning future medical or social care, we involve children in the discussion as much as possible and give them ample opportunity to air their points of view and ask questions.

Informing the school
In conjunction with the children and their parents, we have taken the decision to inform an elected member of staff in the children's schools about their HIV status. Our thinking is governed not by the fact that the school needs to know (indeed, they have no need to know as such) but because the child has a need for someone in the school to know. To send a child to school knowing that he or she must keep their life-threatening condition a secret is, we feel, an unacceptable burden. Far better that he or she can identify members of staff with whom open discussion is possible and who understand the situation and can offer informed care and support. Apart from one adverse reaction from a local school some years ago, this decision has resulted in schools and their staff becoming valuable allies in the continuing care of our children. Follow up at all stages is important in facilitating support for the infected child. Thus, at any critical stage in the child's progress, whether it is the day he or she is informed of their HIV status or a change of school or a significant medical development, the continued support of family and significant others is essential.

Finally, a curious statement but I believe a vital one: be aware of the child's 'wellness' as well as illness. Children, particularly very young children, think on a deep psychological level in terms of very simple polarities. Life is about being good or bad, right or wrong, success or failure. When children come to see us at the hospital our chief concern is usually what is wrong with them. Medically and emotionally, the entire focus of attention is negatively located. To redress the balance we also pay equal attention to what is right with them – from the medical examination at which the doctor makes sure to acknowledge the parts that are working well as well as those that are working not so well, to the counselling situation where I am as eager to hear about the triumphs as about the disasters.

Pre-bereavement counselling

The care and management of children facing bereavement must also be addressed. In Thanet we care for many families where a child is facing or has faced the loss of a parent or sibling. Again, honesty and openness are the cornerstone of our care.

Children's feelings

It is important to prepare children to say goodbye and to participate in the grieving when a family member is terminally ill. One of the most useful tools I have found in preparing children for bereavement is a scrapbook produced by St Christopher's Hospice called *My Book About.* It focuses attention on those areas which I consider significant, in particular, identifying the home as a place to share feelings both happy and sad and therefore encouraging sharing of grief. Many adults still feel that the correct approach to family bereavement is to conceal their own grief, put a brave face on it and carry on as 'normal'. How often I have heard a parent say 'I try not to cry in front of the children', or 'I try not to let them see me upset'. Thus the child becomes isolated with his or her own emotions, and cut off from the right to grieve. I encourage parents to grieve with the children on the basis that crying is OK, it's a good way of letting the pain out. Talking about your feelings is another way of dealing with pain and it is useful to identify people with whom the child can talk, possibly a teacher, a neighbour or a close friend.

We help children to understand the illness, using simple explanations. It is essential that they understand that being ill is not always fatal, that only sometimes, when people are very ill, can the doctors not make them better. We also assure them that the illness is not contagious like chicken pox. We prepare them for the physical changes which may occur such as weight loss, tiredness or incontinence, and especially for the personality changes which may ensue. It is very distressing when mummy suddenly forgets your name or becomes overtly aggressive. We try to differentiate between the 'inside' and the 'outside' person, and that it is only the 'outside' person that has been changed by the illness, the 'inside' person is still shining and beautiful and loves them very much.

Finding a role for them in the illness helps children to have practical ways in which they can express their love. Visiting the sick person, talking to them, carrying a tray to them are all ways of saying how much they care. We also encourage children to visit the ward and spend as much time with the dying relative as possible.

Provision for the future

Practical arrangements play an important part, and can provide parents and children with reassurance for their future existence. The sense of having made adequate provision for one's children's future can bring inner peace to parents. The most valuable assets parents possess are their children, and all parents should make a will and discuss with their children, wherever possible, the future arrangements for their care. In the will they can specify who they wish to have guardianship of their children and the ethnic and religious environment in which they wish them to be brought up. Who will they live with? Who will collect them from school? Who will make their tea? Adequate answers to questions such as these underpin a child's security when faced with separation and loss. I also suggest the idea of treasured keepsakes, identifying some special possession such as a watch or piece of jewellery that is given to the child as a memento, or the writing of a letter which a child can open some time in the future. In it the parent can once again reaffirm love, hopes and wishes for the child, and sadness at missing the important milestones on the child's journey through life. Such a letter can be a life-long treasure, to be read and re-read, a constant link with the parent that death has separated them from.

The idea of a continued existence

'Where do you go when you die?' I have not yet come across a child who does not have some idea of a continued existence after death. The philosophical argument of whether or not there is life after death is irrelevant to the very young. The fact that they find the idea comforting is the fundamental issue, and it does not necessarily require a specific religious context. Innate in all religions is the concept of a heaven-like world to which the soul migrates when physical death occurs. For example, the Christian family has the scenario of a heaven with Jesus and the angels as a setting in which to place the soul. Many families with whom I work, however, have no specific religious beliefs, sometimes none at all, and thus find the religious stereotypes unacceptable. I therefore suggest to them the idea of the 'Summerland', a magical, beautiful garden where the sun is always shining and where there are flowers and trees and birds and little animals to play with. I suggest that children use their imagination or 'inside eyes' to see the Summerland and to visualise the person who has died sitting happily in the magic garden. I encourage children to express their own ideas of how the Summerland might be, and maybe to draw a picture of it.

Metaphysical ideas are failed utterly by their translation into everyday language: the concepts are difficult enough for many adult minds to grasp, let alone a child's. Thus we need a language of interpretation, the language of symbolism. I have already mentioned the 'inside self' and 'the outside self' in expressing the body as distinct from the soul. In explaining death, the symbol of the snail leaving an old and worn shell or the discarding of old clothes which are worn out or too small are useful analogies. Perhaps the best symbolic explanation is one that emanated from a child: when you blow up a balloon you fill it with air, then the balloon bursts and the air inside goes somewhere although you cannot see where, and the tattered balloon that is left is useless and you throw it away.

Whatever our personal beliefs, they are secondary to the needs of a child facing separation by death. Even if the parents are atheist I believe it is not unreasonable to ask them to suspend their atheism to allow the child some comforting imagery in which to accommodate their own impending mortality or that of a family member. Ultimately as the children mature, they will form their own conclusions, as we all do.

The rituals of death

Quite often the first experience of bereavement for a child is the loss of a beloved family pet. The way in which this is handled can set the tone of their whole future approach to death. If the goldfish dies, please don't flush it down the loo – it needs a funeral ceremony as much as any human does – and if the cat has to be put to sleep bring it home from the vet so that the children may see and touch it. Having the opportunity to touch the animal who has died, to love and cuddle it, dig a grave and hold a funeral service facilitates grief; it gives the child the opportunity to experience death as something sad but not frightening.

In a similar way I encourage the families of children where death has occurred, to allow them to experience death. Whether the death takes place at home or in hospital, the ritual of the deathbed is of consequence. In hospital, once the death has occurred, after a little while I take away any family members present at the bedside so that the body can be laid out. It is important that their last memory of the loved person is as beautiful and peaceful as possible without all the indignities of illness, the tubes, the drips, the monitors. Laying the body in an attitude of repose surrounded only by flowers and cards, creates a powerful last impression. The paraphernalia of illness removed, I invite the family to return and remain as long as they wish to say their goodbyes. I encourage the children to be present and to be allowed to touch the body, over which they often display a high degree of curiosity.

Attending the funeral is an important experience for children; they should be allowed to choose whether they wish to attend, but should be given an explanation of what happens at a burial or cremation. The vivid imaginations of the young can produce alarming scenarios. One child imagined his grandfather's funeral would be something akin to the cremation of a Viking War Lord, until the ceremony was explained. Understandably he was initially reluctant to attend. Explain also that a funeral is a time when everyone cries, that there is nothing wrong in getting upset, and that feeling sad is as much a part of life as feeling happy.

Visiting the grave is a significant ritual. While accepting that the 'real' person is not in there, it forms a link, a focus for our thoughts and feelings. They cannot be addressed to thin air, they need a material object for their expression. The child can still make mummy a card on Mother's Day and take it to her grave or tell her of his or her triumphs on sports day. The dialogue with the deceased needs to be continued for as long as the child wants it.

Post-bereavement counselling

Grief produces overwhelming emotion – fear, anger, sadness – the intensity of which can be frightening. It is therefore essential to help children understand these feelings and to experience them as a normal part of grieving. Children need to know that these strange and powerful feelings can last for a long time. Perhaps the most frightening emotion children may experience after a death is that somehow it is their fault, that they have hurt the person in some way, particularly if the death was sudden and there was no time to say goodbye. I remember working with a teenage girl whose sister had died suddenly, and she was having difficulty in coming to terms with the loss. It emerged that there was a great deal of sibling rivalry between the two girls, things had often been said in anger that were never really meant. She was overwhelmed with guilt. A way was needed of expressing the regret and reaffirming her love, and ultimately we settled on the idea of her writing a letter to her sister to express her feelings. Reassurance was also needed that such words of anger between siblings were quite in order and that nothing one says can really hurt anybody.

We all have imaginary conversations in our heads with the living, so why not with those from whom we are separated by death? I encourage children to continue with these conversations and also to visualise the deceased in the Summerland. I suggest that when they go to bed they close their 'outside' eyes and with their 'inside' eyes see mummy or daddy or whoever sitting in the magic garden looking shining and beautiful with a big smile on their face. I ask the child what happens to his or her face at this time (try this yourself). The family can make a scrapbook of photographs and memories together, encouraging and sharing thoughts and feelings.

The last words of the dying Buddha on life were 'it changes'. Our lives are in a constant state of flux, mostly slow imperceptible changes, sometimes sudden and dramatic. Anniversaries are the milestones of our metamorphosis. The first birthday, the first Christmas, the first anniversary of the death are particularly important times. I discuss with the child ways of marking these times – some symbolic action in memory of the person who has died – possibly planting a tree in the garden or making a donation to charity in that person's memory, or any action that they can feel comfortable with. The anniversary is also a time to reflect on the inner change that grief has effected. I talk to the child about the ways they feel they have changed inside or how they feel the people around them have changed.

Change is perhaps the keynote. With regards to the families with whom I work, I do not believe it is my role to challenge the decisions they have taken about their children or the information they have decided to give them. My approach is that the decisions they have taken are the right ones for them at this time. But tomorrow, next week, or next month they may feel differently. And so we must allow for the possibility of change, to have goals to move towards, but to move towards gently, at their own pace. Perhaps death is only another change.

10 The implications of paediatric AIDS for two adoptive families and their children

Sarah Ryan

Sarah Ryan is a social worker for Leeds Social Services. Her initial contact with the two families she describes was made when preparing her dissertation for a master's degree at the University of York, in May 1990.

When I first thought about exploring the issues surrounding the fostering or adoption of children with HIV, it was purely a theoretical concept; I had only read about it and attended a couple of meetings. However, when I visited two families, that concept was translated into a partial understanding of what it meant to live with the uncertainties and challenges of paediatric AIDS. I was faced with the families' dilemmas, frustrations, fears, stresses, pains, hopes and joys, and the impact of AIDS on those families and their children made a marked impression on me.

Many people have not fully realised that a population of children infected by HIV exists, even less how they and their families are affected. This chapter describes the experience of parenting HIV positive children, as relayed to me by two adoptive mothers in Scotland. The accounts are based on open-ended interviews, loosely structured by a series of questions (see Appendix A). It was intended that the adoptive families could identify and discuss the issues that were most important to them as the direct care-givers. My thanks to them both for agreeing to talk to me and for being so enlightening about their experiences and feelings.

For the purposes of confidentiality all the names have been changed.

Routes to the adoption of children who are HIV positive

Mrs F and Billy
Mrs F lives in a sea-side village with her husband and three grown-up adopted sons. She is experienced in short-term fostering, having fostered

up to fifty-eight babies and young children before I met her. When Billy was placed with Mrs F, the social worker told her that it was hoped he would be returned to his birth parents, a plan with which Mrs F was quite comfortable. However, shortly after the placement the social work department decided that Billy was to be made available for adoption. Although Mr and Mrs F were keen to adopt him they were discouraged from doing so at first because of their age.

Billy was a premature baby; Mrs F described him as being happy and cuddly but sickly and difficult and needing a lot of care. During the first few months of placement she noticed that he bruised easily, not just by knocks but even by the cuffs of his cardigan and socks. At a monthly check-up she was assured that there was nothing to be unduly worried about and it wasn't until Billy was a year old that a doctor showed concern at a pre-adoption medical examination. Shortly after this Billy was covered in finger print bruises from the doctor's handling. After some tests Billy's blood platelet level was found to be very low and he was kept in hospital for further tests and a bone-marrow biopsy; his platelet level improved and he was allowed home, to return weekly so that his platelet level could be monitored.

During the following two months Billy remained at home with the Fs until his blood platelet level again caused concern and he stayed in hospital for further tests. Mrs F recounts how confused and devastated she felt at that time and how unsure she was about what they were testing Billy for.

In 1985, at the age of 16 months, Billy was the first baby in Scotland to be identified as HIV positive. For Mrs F, the following two weeks were hard to remember clearly, but her overriding feelings were of fear, confusion and abandonment. She felt that the social work department was in panic, not really sure of what to say or do. The family did not know very much about AIDS, only what they had read in newspapers or seen on TV.

On the first night Billy came home Mrs F told her sons as much as she knew. She was worried about protecting them from infection and anxious because all the boys had played and rolled around with Billy and he had kissed and slobbered over them. Knowing that they had all been in contact with his saliva and she in direct contact with his blood, she was frightened and felt panicked. She was confident that her sons loved Billy very much but didn't know whether his being infected would make them feel any different. The community doctor visited to explain about practical hygiene procedures and generally what was known about paediatric AIDS and risks of infection. Although Mrs F was calmed by this, she was aware that they had already lived in very close contact with Billy for over 16 months without the benefit of this information.

The family talked about what they were going to do. The boys were very sad for Billy and feared he might be locked away. They had visions of his dying in an unfamiliar, lonely place, and they wanted to secure his position in their family. Their application to adopt him was accepted later that year.

Mrs M and Amy

Mr and Mrs M live in the same region with their son John who is now 13 years old. Their route to adoption was quite different from that of the Fs. Mrs M responded to an advertisement in a local paper, describing hard to place children needing adoption. One of them – Amy – was described as an attractive, responsive and affectionate child who unfortunately had two infectious viruses, one of which could be life-threatening. The Ms had never fostered or adopted previously, although they had discussed adoption some time in the past. On reading the advert Mrs M realised that Amy must be infected with HIV.

That evening the Ms discussed what kind of people might take on a child who was HIV positive and likely to die. They thought they would probably be the following :
– people who didn't have any children;
– people who had some medical background;
– people who lived in a city where they could be more anonymous;
– people who lived in a village where they could get support;
– people who lived very near a hospital.
After further consideration they realised that their preconceived ideas were not necessarily right and that:
– other children would be safe;
– they needn't live on the doorstep of a hospital;
– they could live in either a city or a village;
– a medical background wasn't essential.

They started to think about how a child with HIV might affect some aspects of the adopters' lives. How would they be with workmates, friends and family? What would they say to people about the child? How would they behave? How would other people react towards them? How would they cope with illness? Would it affect their ability to continue with their jobs?

Mrs M had a nursing background and continues to work with a Women's Aid group. She knew about HIV infection and drug misuse. She was also aware that women were infected, but like many people she had not, at the time, made the connection that children would also be at risk of HIV infection.

After some discussion the Ms applied to the local social work department and were invited to attend an initial meeting of people who had expressed an interest. When they arrived they expected a room full of people; in fact there were only two other couples besides themselves out of 32 initial responses. They left the information meeting with the onus on them to contact the department.

They duly responded and when their adoption assessment started, they received further information and advice about the practicalities and implications of caring for an HIV infected child. They were not quite prepared for the intensive questioning and counselling involved nor for the attention they received. Although they felt that the social workers were as thorough and informative as possible, due to the lack of previous knowledge and experience they too were unsure of all the issues and implications. (Now the social work department has learnt a great deal and has developed its procedures accordingly.)

The Ms and their social workers explored possible areas of difficulty, including confidentiality, coping with illness, fears about infection, hygiene procedures and uncertainty about life expectancy. (These are discussed in more detail later.) However, information about paediatric AIDS is still developing and new areas for concern continue to arise, and much less was known at that time. The Ms had fears about people rejecting them, fears that Amy would die, and fears about the risk of infection to their son. They gathered information, talked to doctors and social workers, and accepted that the risk of infection to their son was slight and could be prevented by following simple hygiene precautions.

The Ms were approved for adoption and introduced to Amy at her foster home. She was adopted by Mr and Mrs M at the age of two. She is now six years old.

Comment

Probably the most difficult issue for families is the uncertainty about these children's manifestation of illness and their life-expectancy, and the fact that, at present, medical knowledge of the illness is far from comprehensive. Covell wrote in 1987:

> 'A foster or adoptive parent cannot be confidently advised of the chances that a child born to an infected mother will be infected for life; will be more susceptible to infection than a normal child; will suffer from mild or severe clinical manifestations of the disease; or worst will die.'[1]

Adoption is usually a means of increasing the family and it may be very difficult to comprehend the possibility of an early death, especially with an apparently healthy child. Parents need help to confront this and social work and medical staff need to discuss with them the implications for the child, for themselves and their families, in order that they can decide themselves whether or not they can care for an HIV positive child.

Secondly, the diagnosis of HIV infection is a cause for concern. Social workers and doctors should, at the point of diagnosis, present the information sensitively. The response of the carers and the social workers may be one of shock, disbelief, denial and panic. It is very important to discuss with the family the details and symptoms of the illness, and how to use the available resources to treat the illness, emphasising the role the family will play in the total care of the child. Pre- and post-test counselling should be offered to the prospective new parents, particularly when, as in the case of the Fs, a child is already in placement when the diagnosis was made. Sharing with the carers the information which a test for HIV antibodies might yield involves them in the decision-making process and enables them to make more informed decisions.

Thirdly, the adoptive parents often harbour a fear of contagion and risk of infection to themselves and other members of the family and this may recur from time to time in spite of a rational acceptance of evidence to the contrary. Lack of knowledge about the transmission of HIV can leave carers frightened and confused, and can result in social workers offering inconsistent, inconclusive and sometimes misleading advice. It is important that both workers and carers have accurate and up-to-date information about transmission, so that myths can be dispelled. The social worker should establish how much the prospective adoptive parent has already learnt about AIDS and transmission of HIV and should be fully aware of his/her own feelings about it.

Mr and Mrs M had the opportunity to work through their fears and pre-conceived ideas with the help of medical and social service professionals prior to adoption and in a more controlled way than Mr and Mrs F, who had to cope with these fears and anxieties during placement. In any event, carers will require a great deal of support from social work and health services, and co-operation between these two agencies is essential. Counselling before testing and quick and early access to test results is vital.

In both these placements, experience of HIV in children was new to the social workers as well as the parents. The challenge to social work and social workers lies in confronting their own fears and pre-conceived ideas in order to respond appropriately and sensitively. Social workers need to accept that the uncertainties involved naturally cause extra stress and worries for workers as well as carers. Developing a framework of procedures and practice guidelines drawn from experiences so far will help workers who have to deal with these issues in the future.

Confidentiality and what it meant to two adoptive families

Making decisions about who, when and how to tell about a child's HIV status is not easy and presents moral dilemmas. In my interviews with Mrs F and Mrs M, I asked them what confidentiality has meant to them: what were the advantages and disadvantages of keeping strict confidentiality; who had they told and why; what and who had they been advised to tell; and what had been the reactions of people who had been given information about their children's HIV status.

Mrs F

Mrs F reached her difficult decision to disclose Billy's HIV status after talking to her family and Billy's birth mother. The decision was based on the following considerations.

Firstly, Mrs F believes that secrets create stigma and mistrust. She wanted Billy to be brought up knowing that people around him in the community had accepted him in the knowledge that he was HIV positive and that his illness did not stop them liking him. If a child is told that he or she has to be careful what and who he or she tells, then the child will believe that he or she has a terrible illness that cannot be spoken about. Mrs F was concerned that Billy need never be ashamed of being HIV positive.

Secondly, for Mrs F, secrets can leave people feeling trapped and isolated. In many other stressful situations, for instance, those involving illnesses such as leukaemia or cancer, people want to talk about it; they need and want the support and understanding of relatives and friends. With HIV infection and AIDS many people feel they cannot talk and have to struggle on alone. Mrs F knew people who were afraid to tell for fear of rejection.

Another and more contentious reason for the disclosure was the responsibility that Mrs F felt towards others who came into regular contact with Billy. When he started playgroup Mrs F informed the staff that he was HIV positive. She was aware that the staff did not wear plastic gloves for playground accidents and she felt that whoever was looking after Billy (including other parents working at the playgroup) should know how to protect themselves, other children, and Billy. Although the chances of an accident happening were very slim, Mrs F didn't want to take the risk of other adults or children being exposed to infected blood. Although this is no longer a reason for disclosure as good standards of general hygiene are known to provide adequate protection, Mrs F also felt that the playgroup could help Billy, who, by then, was developing symptoms and who was therefore susceptible to infection from other children.

The staff and parents involved in the playgroup met with Mrs F who told them what she knew about the illness, the risk of infection, the routes of transmission, and hygiene precautions that could be employed. The staff then consulted the health clinic who reiterated and confirmed what Mrs F had told them regarding the low risk of infection. Billy joined the playgroup and Mrs F has been supported by them and by the school he attended afterwards. The staff watched out for when Billy had a cold and were sensitive to when he felt he could not participate. Mrs F was reassured by this mutual co-operation and support.

The wider community also responded supportively. Billy played with neighbours' children and went on trips with them. By telling people in the community Mrs F felt that she and Billy had more freedom, and some of their stresses and anxieties were lessened. She is aware that the issue is more complex but she is grateful for the positive reaction in their community.

At the time, the social work department and the doctors were not in complete agreement with Mrs F. She was advised about the disadvantages of talking openly to people. However, Mrs F found that, with access to knowledge and information, the people amongst whom she and Billy lived were very understanding of her situation. She suggests that local centres should offer advice and information to people in the community in order to dispel myths and fears.

When Billy had been placed for some time, he and Mrs F had a considerable amount of media exposure to show people that living with an HIV positive child does not prevent a family from leading a normal life, and in the hope that the public might develop a better understanding of HIV infection and AIDS. Mrs F is presently making a teaching video for her local social work department which will be shown to people interested in fostering or adopting an HIV positive child.

Mrs M

Mrs M felt that her own and Amy's right to choose to keep the infection confidential was usurped. Initially it was easy to maintain confidentiality within the boundaries of the immediate family. However, when Amy was three years old and Mrs M wanted to enrol her at the local playgroup, problems arose. Mrs M was aware that the playgroup had received guidelines concerning appropriate hygiene procedures with regards to preventing transmission of HIV infected blood, but found that the guidelines were not being employed. Her first reaction was to enrol Amy anyway as it was the playgroup's responsibility to protect all the children, including Amy, from risk of infection. However, she personally felt she had a moral responsibility to protect all the children attending the playgroup.

Mrs M met with the playgroup leaders, expecting that their reaction would be to tighten up their hygiene procedures. Instead, a committee decided that all the other parents had a right to be informed. Mrs M argued strongly that if the proper hygiene procedures were in operation for all children then nobody would be at risk and confidentiality could be maintained. She argued further that the playgroup should be implementing the appropriate hygiene precautions regardless, because of the eventuality of there being an undiagnosed child with HIV infection in the group. She felt that Amy's right to confidentiality was being denied because of people's irrational fear of infection and belief in their own right to know.

Mrs M knew that Amy would benefit from being at a playgroup and she felt she had to accept the committee's decision for that reason, and also because the confidentiality she sought had, because of living in a small village community, already been breached. Both Mrs M and the playgroup leaders contacted agencies that could offer advice and information about the risks of infection and appropriate hygiene precautions.

The days following the breach of Amy's medical privacy were hard. Mrs M felt anger, fear, pain and distress because she did not know who knew, and she had to force herself to face people in the community. She continued to emphasise the importance of proper hygiene for all children regardless of their HIV status. She feels that a contradiction occurs because although guidelines suggest that all children should be treated as if they were 'at risk' of being infected with HIV, they are not adhered to unless there is knowledge of a child who is HIV positive already being present. Mrs M was frustrated to find that when Amy moved on from the playgroup, they had ceased to implement the hygiene procedures.

Mrs M felt that although there are times when it may be necessary and beneficial to relax confidentiality, that should be the individual's choice. She was also concerned for birth parents who might, for their own reasons, need to maintain confidentiality. It is easier for adoptive parents because the adopted child is seen as an innocent victim and the adoptive family consequently receives sympathy and support, while birth parents may be blamed, rejected and lose their support network.

The Ms felt, however, that it was only fair to explain about Amy's illness to their son John. Mrs M named it Hepatitis B at first and told him what he needed to do when Amy was bleeding. They feel that their son is well informed and has accepted the situation well. They helped him rehearse his own answers to potentially difficult questions. When information about Amy leaked into the community, John moved to a secondary school in a different area so that he would have an outlet, a place where friends didn't know that his sister had the HIV virus.

The Ms have also had a high media exposure. Having lost their confidentiality Mrs M feels that now they can present the case for other people's right to maintain confidentiality, and hopefully begin to change people's attitudes towards these children.

Comment

Confidentiality is an emotive issue. In 1988, Reamer said: 'A client's right to confidentiality is among the most enduring and sacred social work values.'[2] However, the AIDS crisis has forced social work departments to test the traditional limits of this right as the consequences of a too rigid or too open approach to confidentiality can have a detrimental effect on the child, the child's family and the local community.

The burning question concerning a child's HIV status is who needs to know? Do schools/playgroups need to know? Do parents of other foster children in a home need to know? Do their social workers need to know? Do siblings need to know? Do childminders need to know? Does anyone who comes to the house need to know?

Foster parents are familiar with the issue of confidentiality but HIV presents new problems. The choice can either be one of painful isolation or rejection if a child's HIV status is made public knowledge. The issue is partly determined by the possible or likely reactions of the surrounding community, whose response to AIDS and HIV infection will determine the degree of support available, and the chances of preventing further transmission of infection. In both Billy's and Amy's cases, difficulties were experienced by both parents when their children joined a playgroup.

Although there has been no documentation of HIV transmission in schools, daycare and other settings, and despite guidelines in Britain and the USA specifying that children who are HIV positive can be included in the classroom, the education of such children has been an emotionally charged topic, particularly with regard to the right to confidentiality.

Mrs F felt that giving information is one way of combating negative reactions, and earlier, suggested that information should be made accessible at a local level. Education about transmission of the virus is important for a better understanding. Both Mrs F and the social work department, and Mrs M, who is involved in formulating an AIDS training programme for use in schools, believe that education is an important factor in how people perceive HIV positive people, in preventing HIV transmission, in facilitating appropriate hygiene precautions and thereby in providing the opportunity to choose who needs to know the child's HIV status.

Living with a child who is HIV positive

What are the difficulties of day-to-day living with a child who is HIV positive? Mrs F and Mrs M's accounts encompassed four main issues: support, coping with illnesses and treatment, what to say to the child about his/her infection, and facing the future and the possibility of bereavement.

Mrs F and Billy

Support: Mrs F had a positive reception from her local community. She enjoyed and was comforted by the support they provided. Her family shared the workload and the anxieties, and, she added, the pleasure of caring for Billy. She is confident that when Billy was at school people understood his illness and were sensitive to his good and bad periods. She had a supportive relationship with the nurses and other medical staff and had access to the paediatrician, Dr Jackie Mok, who explained Billy's treatment and listened to her worries about illness and development. She attended a support group in an Edinburgh clinic for parents of children who were, or are, at risk of being HIV positive.

Coping with illness and treatment: Mrs F took Billy to the clinic at the Edinburgh hospital every three weeks for his infusion of gamma globulin to boost his immune system against bacterial infection. She found the hospital visits depressing, despite the friendly and helpful attitude of the nursing staff because the reality of the progression of his illness was emphasised.

Billy was given AZT (zidovudine) and was also on a long-term course of antibiotics. Often Mrs F could not determine whether he was nauseous because of the side-effects of medication, the HIV virus, or some ordinary illness of childhood, and not knowing was frustrating.

At first Billy suffered from lengthy colds, nausea and cramps in his legs. Mrs F avoided too much fuss. If he had cramps she rubbed his legs, if he was cold she put on extra sweaters. Billy began to lose his balance, fall over and walk into things. He was a boy of spirit and seldom complained. He continued with gymnastics and swimming when he wanted to. At this time Mrs F felt that he wasn't severely ill.

Talking to Billy about his illness: Initially Billy was brought up to believe that the virus he had was a cold virus. He knew it could make him very ill and he knew that some people with the virus had died. Following a school campaign and a TV programme, he also knew that there were children and babies in Romania who had the same virus, some of whom are extremely ill and dying, but that those children did not have the money or medication to make them better.

Gradually (according to his age and understanding) Billy learnt more about his own illness and himself. He knew that he mustn't let other people touch his blood because he could catch viruses from them and they could catch viruses from him. He knew that people at school or those who took him out, etc, should have a first-aid bag containing cotton wool, elastoplasts and disposable gloves. Mrs F did not discourage Billy from talking about his illness and asking her questions about going to the hospital and, more painfully for her, about dying.

Facing the future and the possibility of bereavement: In March 1990, when asked about the future, Mrs F told me that the doctors thought Billy was going to die. People asked her if she was prepared for Billy's death and she felt that nobody really knew whether he would die or not. This made her angry.

When Billy was ill, inert, had a high temperature and was bruising easily, the uncertainty depressed her. She managed on a day-to-day basis, and tried to learn more about different ways of coping from the medical staff and from other parents in her support group.

For a short time the use of steroids improved the quality of Billy's life. In August 1990, the medical staff discovered a tumour in his leg and the Fs had difficult decisions to make about the appropriate type of medical treatment. Mrs F felt that Billy looked so healthy, and was consequently very confused.

When the doctors told her that they could do no more for Billy, she felt frustrated and angry. She had not noticed the deterioration in the child that others could see. He had dropped one and a half stones in weight but had grown several inches. She was unable to hold or cuddle him for months because of the pain he suffered.

In March 1991, when almost seven years old, Billy died. He was at home with his adoptive parents who were then able to hold and cuddle him. With the help of Mrs F, Billy had found his own way of talking about dying and before he died he told his mum that he was going to heaven. The whole of the community paid tribute to him at his cremation. Mrs F has felt more able to cope with her loss because of this support.

Mrs M and Amy

Support: Throughout the adoption assessment, Mrs M and her family received information, counselling and support from the social work department and other professionals. Later they were supported by their immediate family and found that once friends had an opportunity to examine the facts about HIV, particularly its transmission, they were sympathetic and supportive.

Unfortunately, the battle with the playgroup resulted in many people in the local community regarding Amy as a kind of imported HIV positive child and did not seriously consider HIV infection as relevant to themselves. However, more recently, many people in the community became actively supportive towards the whole family. Mrs M considered the hospital staff to be her main support; there, she felt that she could 'dump' her fears and anxieties about Amy's illness and the uncertainty of the future. She appreciated access to Amy's medical notes and test results and the opportunity to discuss these.

Coping with illness and treatment: Adapting to day-to-day life with Amy was fairly easy and straightforward despite being led to believe it would be difficult. Amy's clothes were washed with everybody else's, she used the same cutlery, plates, etc, and the same toilet. When she cut herself she came to her mother who put on plastic gloves, mopped up the blood with cotton wool, put a waterproof elastoplast on the cut, and then put the gloves and cotton wool in a disposable bag. When they went out Mrs M took an emergency pack with her.

On my last visit, Mrs M felt that Amy was generally quite well. She gets conjunctivitis, diarrhoea, 'flu, thrush, colds, coughs and tummy upsets. The symptoms can be treated but they tend to last three or four weeks. Amy has a lot of viral infections which are long lasting and hard to treat. She gets bacterial infections less often and these can be treated with antibiotics. Sometimes Amy's continuing minor illnesses are tiring and demanding but the family takes them as they come. They are conscious that the big one could come along at any time, although most of the time they do not think about it. Mrs M takes Amy to the clinic in Edinburgh every three weeks for a gamma globulin infusion. She tries to prevent Amy coming into contact with children who have been exposed to chicken pox and other infections for which there is no vaccination.

Living with an HIV positive child is limiting in unexpected ways. You must consider carefully whether or not you can go to work, use a childminder, go on holidays abroad, and must be permanently conscious of hygiene procedures.

Talking to Amy about her illness: Amy knows she has 'germs' in her blood which emerge when she bleeds and she doesn't let other children near her blood. She knows that other 'germs' can infect her blood from other people. She knows that she has to go to hospital for medicine which prevents the 'germs' from making her ill. She is aware that people aren't always comfortable with her and Mrs M has had to explain to her that sometimes other people don't understand that her 'germs' only come out when she bleeds. Although Amy doesn't fully understand what her illness is, she learns more as she asks more questions.

Facing the future and the possibility of bereavement: The progression of infection in Amy is monitored and nobody can be sure how long she will live. When I last visited, Mrs M believed that she has a lot of life left. The family treat Amy as normally as possible and do not encourage people to spoil her unduly. After all she might grow into a spoilt teenager! They try not to think too often about the future; whether Amy will live to enjoy adolescence and have sexual relationships, or whether she will deteriorate rapidly. The family live for today, or for this week, and say they will worry about uncertainties when they become reality.

Comment

From these two accounts of living with Billy and Amy, both practical and emotional implications emerge.

First, good hygiene should always be observed and should become a way of life (NFCA have produced guidelines[3] about precautions to be taken when caring for HIV positive children). It is also necessary to consider whether all members of the family are capable of following the procedures for themselves.

Additionally, caring for an HIV positive child involves regular trips to hospital. As Mrs F described, the first hospitalisation was a highly distressing experience. Subsequent hospital visits are no less distressing particularly when they involve confronting the reality of a progressive illness and the development of new symptoms. A good relationship with medical staff is important in order to benefit fully from advice about coping with anxieties over changes in a child's health.

Regarding the emotional implications, uncertainty about the changing nature of the illness is demanding. Tiblier et al[4] suggest that continual role changes are required of everyone involved – family, social workers, school staff and health workers. The child may have stable periods of varying lengths alternating with periods of medical crisis. The family can attempt to carry on with its normal routine, as Mrs F and Mrs M preferred to do, but the spectre of crisis continually looms. Support is vital to the caring families who will choose their own support networks. Mrs F's main support was the community whilst Mrs M's was the hospital staff. The role for social workers is to identify possible support systems and to remain available to the family.

When and what Mrs F and Mrs M decided to tell Billy and Amy about their HIV status was sometimes dictated by actual events, but primarily based on what they felt their children could understand at a particular time, according to their ages. Hepworth and Shernoff[5] put forward two age-appropriate strategies for talking with children about HIV and AIDS. For pre-school children (0 – 4 years) a parent can create an atmosphere in which children learn to feel free to ask any questions about their bodies, health, sexuality. This lays the groundwork for open, honest discussion that can continue in later years.

Early school-age children (5 – 9 years) can absorb fairly complicated concepts about life. Thus, if a child cuts him/herself this may be a time to explain how things that can make you sick can get into your blood, and we all have to be very careful.

In order to be able to talk to children it is obviously important to know and understand them. Mrs F's relationship with Billy enabled her to talk to him about heaven and about dying. When I first met Mrs F and Mrs M, both children appeared to be relatively well and healthy looking and the possibility of bereavement was something that neither mother felt able to confront. Both felt better able to cope and to support their children by dealing with their illness on a day-to-day basis, focusing their attention on providing Billy and Amy with a good quality of life in the present.

This attitude prevailed, so that both women seemed to express a form of denial, partly because, in Billy's case, Mrs F didn't see gradual deterioration and in Amy's case, there has been a long period of remission. This may also have been because denial was in itself a prop enabling them to support their children.

Families caring for HIV positive children live with uncertain knowledge about whether their child might die. Social workers must be prepared to support families in their current attitude to this, to find strategies which enable them to keep going, and, ultimately, to be prepared for bereavement counselling.

Family placement of children who are infected with HIV is not all doom and gloom, anxiety and fear. Mrs F and Mrs M have experienced many moving and happy times and both knew that they were contributing to the well being of children when others would not or could not. Those of us working in social services can learn from their experiences in order to prepare for our responsibilities for such children in the future.

References

1 Covell, Dr R G, 'HIV infection and adoption in Scotland', *Scottish Medical Journal*, p17, August 1987.

2 Reamer, F G, *AIDS and clinics: the agenda for social work*, Vol 33, p 401, Sep/Oct 1988.

3 National Foster Care Association, *AIDS & HIV: information for foster carers*, NFCA, 1987.

4 Tiblier et al, Macklin (ed), *AIDS & Families: Report of the AIDS task force*, Groves conference on marriage and the family, Harrington Park Press, 1989.

5 Hepworth J and Shernoff M, Macklin (ed) as 4. above, p.73.

11 Sharing my home with positive people

Sue Wates

Sue Wates is a social worker by training and is the adoptive mother of four, now all young adults. She works closely with the London Lighthouse and Positive Options projects to help families affected by HIV.

When I was first asked by a friend to care for a man who was terminally ill with complications caused by the AIDS virus, I was not at all sure that it was something I wanted to do. Following my mother's death, I had kept in place the facilities that enabled us to care for her at home but AIDS was not something that I knew anything about, beyond the general doom and gloom of the tombstone splitting publicity, nor were gay men a group that I felt particularly at home with.

At the time, trying to obtain practical, first-hand knowledge was not easy for me; I did not know where to start. I do not mind admitting that I was extremely fearful of what might be involved and I particularly wanted to talk to another 'housewife and mother' who could tell me the truth about cups and saucers and lavatory seats. Rather by accident, I found myself talking to the community care workers at London Lighthouse and before I knew it, I found that I had volunteered to offer holidays to people with the virus, so I had to gain some knowledge pretty quickly. This I did by reading the available literature and joining a Lighthouse group for the family and friends of people affected by the virus.

The first person who came to stay was a marvellous introduction and from him I learned much about what it was like growing up and realising that you are gay. I also learned about his coming to terms with the virus, experiencing the negative side but also the positive: grief about the possibility of an early death, but at the same time the chance to put his life in order and find support through Lighthouse and the friends he met there. Getting to know him changed my attitude and one day I realised, when I thought that someone might have brought chicken pox into our home, that I had overcome my fear of HIV because I had discovered that I was far more of a danger to him than he to me.

What I can offer

I had always said that I would like to offer holidays to families. With my social work background I hoped that I could be of real help in talking with women and children about what was happening to them. From my first family, again, I learned so much. Penny was a drug addict with two lively, attractive children, who came for a week with John, a new partner who was recently diagnosed HIV+ and who was extremely depressed by the discovery, having seen a man with whom he used to share a needle die a very painful death. Penny's life had been a catalogue of unhappiness: she had been sexually abused as a child, she had also been raped, she had parted with a child for adoption, had been widowed twice, and had many years of drug abuse. She was now trying to make something of the life that she had left to her, but since her status had become known, she suffered rejection at the hands of her family as well as friends and neighbours. Different arrangements were made each time for her children and she had a great worry about what would happen to them upon her death. She had no one with whom she could talk about her children's future.

This problem of no-one to talk to was echoed by others who came to stay: Mary, a divorced mother bringing up two children on her own, contracted the virus from a chance sexual encounter at a party and was so stunned by the diagnosis that she could talk to no-one except medical personnel. Faith was a refugee from Africa, with no family in Britain except the daughter with whom she had arrived. Fred's family and that of his children's mother were in Ireland and he was totally dependent on the many London agencies for people with AIDS. Michelle was a drug addict and had never had the care of her daughter who was being raised by Michelle's mother, but she wanted to have a holiday to remember, with her child, before she became too ill. Interestingly, out of the ten 'bookings' in 1991, only two were from gay men.

I am able to offer families their own self-contained accommodation within my house, with its own sitting room, etc. The guests usually make their own breakfast and snack lunch, and I cook an evening meal. On Sundays we all eat with whoever else is staying in my house (my adult children or friends and relations). I make a point of telling them I am a 'Neighbours' fan and we watch it together as that provides an easy occasion for a chat, besides the other times when we meet around the place. There is a communicating door into my part of the house so that they can pop in and out. This is particularly reassuring for the children and enables me to keep an ear open for anything they might need help with – one evening I had to go in when things seemed to be getting out of hand with Michelle and her daughter; another night I got it wrong and they were having a great time playing hide and seek!

In working with people with AIDS great stress is laid by the experts on the need for workers to have come to terms with their own sexuality and death. As someone who is finding middle age a time of rich harvest, I hope I have dealt with the former. I certainly find it a great help that I walked very closely in the valley of the shadow of death with a brother and a sister-in-law; that experience as well as mourning their deaths was of great value, particularly in dealing with the untimely deaths of young people who still have so much to live for.

Some observations

In my limited experience, what comes over above all is how hard a time all the women are having. They are clearly much more worried about preserving their anonymity than are gay men; the supportive networks of women are in neighbourhoods where other women are less likely to have come to terms with their fears of the virus than have men supported by the gay networks. The sense of isolation in Mary, for instance, was quite devastating. A good focus for supportive work is to try to help women to identify potentially supportive friendships. For fear of rejection, women can be very wary of telling others and they may need more practical help from agencies than other groups, yet at the same time they may feel inhibited at first from using them. Confidentiality is an important issue and women are much more worried about being recognised than men and this may inhibit them from using support. Drug users may have had a very chaotic lifestyle and winning their trust can be difficult. Quite often when my visitors arrive, they are bewildered by the new surroundings; I find that a great ice-breaker and trust-builder is to ask them to hold or mind my small grand-daughter.

The feeling of guilt is very evident from having put both themselves and their children at risk of a potentially fatal disease. Anger and hurt are difficult emotions to work with and I am sure must often get projected onto helping agencies who will never get everything right, no matter how hard they try. Mourning and grieving for one's own death when one has dependent children is very painful: when Mary trusted me enough to express her feelings, the fact that I cried with her seemed to be very helpful. Because people with the virus see its often very distressing outcome in hospital, the recognition of early signs of the virus starting to affect the brain can be very frightening.

Every one of my guests has had a terrible tale to tell of people's reaction to their HIV status: of rejection, of blame, of malicious graffiti, of the killing of family pets (their bodies being left where the children would find them) and of sheer ignorance in hospitals and dentists' surgeries. Once people reach centres of excellence they are treated with real care and respect, but if the diagnosis is made in a hospital unfamiliar with all aspects of treatment for those infected with HIV, the sufferer is sometimes treated far from compassionately. This is more likely to happen to women who may not be so alert to the risk of HIV infection as gay men, and are therefore less likely to be well informed about where to go for treatment.

I have noticed that children are by and large very protective of a sick parent. The children who have stayed with me along with their parents have also needed a lot of unspoken reassurance that it is safe to be with them on holiday, and from time to time they have needed to make sure that I am around. When we have been doing things together, the children have all, without exception, told me of their love for their mothers, and have wanted to be assured that I genuinely liked them too. I have found it very important to touch them rather more than an English person would normally do! Because they face so much ignorance about how the virus is passed on, I try to build up their confidence so that they believe in the knowledge that I have.

Once a family affected by the virus does get into the supportive network, it can become a complete new way of life. Then, suddenly, they discover the existence of people (such as those at London Lighthouse, the Terrence Higgins Trust, and all the 'Positivelys') who are supportive and helpful. What I try to offer is a caring place where they are truly welcome, where their illness is accepted but where they will have the chance to mix with people whose whole lives are not bound by involvement with the virus. I should add that people other than those affected by the virus also stay with me, and what people say to my other guests here is up to them. I hope that my home feels like a safe place where they can relax and be accepted.

The first time that one of the mothers on methadon maintenance started speaking, as I then thought inappropriately, about what would happen to the children when she died, I made the mistake of saying perhaps we could talk about this later, meaning without the children. I have now developed enough confidence to realise that this is a question that is uppermost in the entire family's mind and it is more reassuring to the children if it can be discussed openly and without undue denial.

I try to give the families time to talk if they want to, and, very importantly, to have fun together so that when the parent becomes increasingly ill or dies, there will be a stock of happy memories to look back on. I make a point of taking lots of photos. There is generally fun and laughter and I try and share the care of the children so that the mother can have a good rest, and to be around for the children when the parents are perhaps tired or sleepy. I have a rule that I will not take anyone who is injecting, for obvious reasons, and have had no difficulty with people on methadon maintenance.

It is very different to be a hostess as distinct from a social worker. When I am asked to take someone in for a holiday, I know little about them – what they tell me is up to them and has varied greatly. I have been moved when they have shared their pain and fears with me, and when they have wanted to come back. Penny needed respite care; her children returned to their regular foster mother and she chose to come to me rather than go into hospital. Penny is now one of the lucky ones: social services have found a family willing to take the children on a regular basis and who accept their need for constant reassurance when parted from her.

Looking back over the changes in myself and my life over the past two years since I first became involved with people infected and affected by the virus, I feel very fortunate to have been able to share my home in this way and I know that in coming to terms with my own fears, ignorance and prejudice, I have become a better person. All my guests have had a tale to tell of trying to come to terms with terrible life-threatening illness, not only for themselves, but also for their families. Besides having to accept their own internal world and possibly impending death, they have had to do this in a society full of ignorance and prejudice. I have been impressed by their courage and fortitude and by how hard they have tried to do their best for their children in the face of such overwhelming difficulty. Of great importance to me has been the fact that I am working with organisations that I respect and trust, and knowing that if I ever got out of my depth, they would be there to help me.

In summary, on the basis of having lived under the same roof as people with HIV and AIDS I would like to share some conclusions. Firstly, I believe that in order to survive well, you have to start with coming to terms with your fear and ignorance. Once this has been achieved, if you feel well supported both by a personal network and the HIV network, coping is possible. It does not mean that mistakes won't happen, but it does mean that you can act with confidence. The wider social work issues seem to be concerned with trying to identify supportive friendship networks for women and their families, ensuring that as much practical help as possible is made available to the families. Because of the general hostility to HIV, confidentiality needs to be thought through on a basis of the 'need to know'. It is very important that social services respond on more than an ad hoc basis to the mothers' need for help in dealing with the longer term planning issues for their children. This has to be done with enormous sensitivity and it is encouraging to know that a body of expertise is being built up in Positive Options (see Chapters 6 and 7), the service set up by Barnardo's for families affected by HIV and AIDS, and indeed in all other agencies which are now starting to have more women and children using their resources. We do not need to be out there re-inventing the wheel on our own: there are people we can turn to for help and guidance, and for our own support.

12 Meeting the challenge:
An agenda for agencies

Daphne Batty

Daphne Batty is co-ordinating Secretary of the BAAF Medical Group. Formerly she managed adoption and fostering services in two London Boroughs.

Summary of current developments

In the UK we must be grateful for the fact that, for whatever reason, HIV infection has not spread as rapidly as was feared in the mid-1980s. But the statistics charting the development of the disease show that it is spreading inexorably into the heterosexual population and will continue to do so for some years to come. While, as stated in Chapter 2, there is still some justification for identifying children born into certain sections of the population as likely to be at greater risk of infection, this may no longer be justifiable in ten years time.

Although neither full protection from the disease nor a cure for it is by any means imminent, the development of prophylactic treatment to modify symptoms has run parallel with the growth of the infection. This has led to an adjustment in attitudes to the testing of children by agencies in areas where the incidence is greatest, and the 'received' view in these agencies seems now to be that outlined by Dr Newell and Professor Peckham in the final paragraph of Chapter 2. This is that testing may be of benefit to children born to fathers known to be bisexual, or where either parent abuses drugs intravenously or has lived in a country where the disease is endemic. The same applies to children known to have been abused by anyone from these groups.

The golden rule, however, continues to be that *each child must be considered individually, taking into account all the circumstances in every case.* These include not only the views of the child's birth parents and carers, but also, as Simmy Viinikka has clearly demonstrated in Chapter 4, the views of children old enough to understand their situations.

The fact that many asymptomatic children are distressed by regular hospital monitoring of their infection must also be taken into account.

How agencies are responding

Contributors to this book have shown that some agencies, both statutory and voluntary, have responded to the challenge and have developed imaginative and far-reaching policies. Others have done little. One large inner city agency looking after many hundreds of children, said in 1986 that their statisticians had estimated that the chances of their dealing with an HIV infected child were minimal and did not merit priority service. This attitude is understandable in these days of resource rationing, but, apart from the fact that a highly vulnerable child would receive an ill-prepared and probably fragmented service, the increasing numbers of non-infected but acutely affected children were not reckoned with at all.

Because early referrals of children were from drug abusing families and the response of agencies to this need was immediate, thorough and well publicised, children at risk of HIV still tend to be thought of as invariably coming from families with a chaotic lifestyle. But as Joan Fratter shows in Chapter 7, an increasing proportion of affected children come from families, including those from some parts of Africa, which have previously made no call on any supportive agency and who are now keen and able to make the best possible plans for their children. Unless support is made available to them, in some cases their lifestyles could degenerate into chaos.

All community health authorities and some social services departments have specialist workers with extensive knowledge of adult HIV infection and AIDS, and they are active in promoting staff training. Many of them, but not all, are alert to the need to extend their knowledge to cover child development as they become more involved with HIV infected women. On the other hand, social workers mainly involved with children are often ignorant of the implications of HIV infection in adults. Cross fertilisation is required and should not be too difficult to establish. Barnardo's Positive Options provides a model in, for instance, seconding a child care social worker to the self-help agency, Positively Women.

An agenda for an agency response

Outlined below is an agenda which we believe should be addressed by all agencies whose responsibilities include working with children and their families.

1 *Agency managements* should acknowledge, regardless of whether or not there is presently a high incidence of HIV infection in their area, that, sooner or later, they will be dealing with infected families and consequently with both infected and affected children.

2 *Training schemes* are required for a wide range of staff, including residential social workers and foster carers and also prospective adopters. These schemes should include the various degrees of both adult and paediatric infection – asymptomatic, symptomatic and AIDS itself – and their implications for family life, including the affected children. Issues regarding confidentiality and consent to treatment, as set out in Chapter 4, should also be covered. Training should acknowledge that there will inevitably be hidden incidence of infection in both adults and children. All training should fulfil the requirements of the Children Act 1989 that consideration must be given to children's racial, cultural, religious and linguistic backgrounds.

3 *Statutorily required standards of hygiene*, wherever children are cared for, should be strictly maintained. Agency policy should include the monitoring of standards of hygiene in the homes of foster carers and prospective adopters, emphasising that there can be no absolute guarantee that children will be free of infection.

4 *Responsibility for updating information* on HIV and AIDS should be invested in a named member of staff who could collate relevant specialist information from within the agency, for example, from drug abuse or family placement workers, and from outside, for instance, from the community health authority, the health education authority, specialist voluntary agencies and HIV newsheets.

5 *Information about medical advice* available in the agency should be given to all workers. This could include the following:
– The adoption agency's medical adviser, who is required by the Adoption Agencies Regulations 1983 to be named and to be a member of the agency's adoption panel. He or she should have specialist knowledge of child development and has responsibility for collating the

health needs of each child from the time of referral until an adoption order is made.

– Medical advice required by the Children Act 1989 (section 27) to be made available to local authorities by health authorities regarding interpreting medical reports, assisting in arrangements for health care and in child care decisions. Unfortunately there is no statutory requirement for this to be provided by a named doctor, but wisely, rather than providing advice on an ad hoc basis, many agencies do extend the duties of the adoption adviser to include all children being looked after.

– A medical adviser employed directly by the local authority. He or she will be expected to advise on a wide range of health issues and is unlikely to be a specialist in child health, although possibly knowledgeable regarding adult AIDS. Workers unaware of the paediatric specialism available to a local authority may approach the local authority adviser in the first instance.

– Medical advisers to agencies who are statutorily nominated under the adoption agencies regulations or performing duties under the Children Act should identify specialists in paediatric AIDS in their areas who would be available for consultation as required. They should also ensure that any medical adviser employed directly by the local authority is aware of their role and responsibilities regarding children looked after by the authority.

6 *Legal advisers* should be included in training provision and should be knowledgeable about, and particularly sensitive to, issues of confidentiality and consent when proffering advice regarding HIV affected children.

7 *Voluntary agencies in the area* relevant to HIV/AIDS should be identified and personal contact made. As indicated by Hong Tan in Chapter 8, some of these agencies were not set up to serve families but will welcome training in child care so that their service provision can be adapted. Others offer support groups with whom family members can quickly identify. The high degree of personal experience concentrated in these agencies offers invaluable insight for social workers with affected families.

8 *The pros and cons of testing for HIV infection* should be discussed in principle by management and included in all staff training. If an agency

policy is drawn up, this should always allow for adjustments in the light of increasing knowledge of the disease and should be reviewed at least annually, in consultation with the agency's medical adviser and local specialist medical knowledge.

9 *The decision whether or not to test* a child born to infected parents, or an abused child, or a young person at risk through sexual activity should always be on an individual basis, taking all the circumstances into account including the wishes and feelings of the child or young person. Consideration should also be given to whether or not it would be preferable for the adults involved to be tested, providing this is practicable and the appropriate counselling is available.

10 *Flexible services for families* are essential as the prime purpose in most cases will be for children to remain at home for as long as possible. Solutions are often dictated by individual needs. Joan Fratter gives some examples in Chapter 7 and points out opportunities presented by the Children Act. Strict adherence to procedures originally designed for circumstances differing from those appertaining to HIV can inhibit imaginative responses to family problems.

11 *Preparation of foster and adoptive families* should include information about HIV/AIDS (see paragraphs 2 and 3 above). It should be borne in mind that different qualities in carers may be required when caring for infected children from those required when caring for affected children. The former will need regular hospital treatment, will be likely to be very ill from time to time and may well die, whereas the latter will be experiencing the serious illness of a parent, often frequent absences from home and possibly the loss of a parent. They may also have to face the loss of a sibling, with the additional stress caused by their parents' attention and caring services having been focused on the sick child.

Wherever possible, preparation should involve contact with families experienced in caring for children at risk of HIV, and Lothian carers have said that access to a Parents' Group has given them an insight into the difficulties encountered by HIV families themselves.

12 *Support for carers* should be given high priority. In the first place, this must mean named social work and medical support being readily available to the carer, including outside office hours (we have no record of abuse of such a service). Membership of a group of carers of infected

or affected children is greatly valued. Respite care and the identification of personal support for carers should be built into placement planning.

13 *Confidentiality* is a complex issue in all work with children separated from their birth families. In the case of HIV affected families the stigma which lingers on around the condition adds to the complexity. Stigma inhibits some families from confronting the implications of infection, while the increasing possibility of prophylactic treatment makes confrontation desirable. Gerry O'Hara in Chapter 5 addresses this issue from the social work agency point of view, and Simmy Viinikka in Chapter 4 examines the legal issues, while Sarah Ryan in Chapter 10, describing the very different approaches of two adoptive mothers, demonstrates that there is no standard response to cover all circumstances. Carol Lindsay Smith, in Chapter 6, advises a brief written statement which explains what confidentiality actually means in this context, clarifies who needs to be told, what to record and how much detail to share with colleagues and in meetings.

Experienced agencies now seem to agree upon the basis of a 'need to know' approach, and that a policy of informing schools and nurseries about asymptomatic children could distract from the real situation, which is that any child could be infected. From the early days of family placement of 'at risk' children most agencies have accepted that carers should know, and that general practitioners and health visitors should be notified. Parents should be kept informed of any intended sharing of this information and their co-operation sought unless there are clear reasons against this which relate to the welfare of the child. The imparting of such knowledge should always be accompanied by the provision of support, as outlined in paragraph 11 above. This should include ensuring that the GP and the health visitor have access to specialist medical advice.

14 *School children* infected or affected by HIV are especially vulnerable to the effects of stigma. They may be subjected to questions about family illness while having to keep their family's secrets.

Support should be available to them, ensuring that as far as possible they have accurate knowledge about their own and their family's situation and about the help that can be offered. They need a safe space in which they can ask questions and express feelings without risk of breach of confidentiality.

15 *Bereavement counselling* should be an integrated part of the support services available to families and to those working with them. The need for this cannot be solely confined to parents and children; grandparents and other relatives may have to care for terminally ill children and grandchildren while at the same time looking after healthy young family members. Judith Swindells in Chapter 9 and Sue Wates in Chapter 11, together with workers in children's hospices throughout the country contribute to a growing body of experience in bereavement work.

Conclusion

This chapter has attempted to review some of the issues raised in the previous chapters and to summarise their implications for child care agencies. Workers in the field of HIV are constantly meeting new challenges and we are grateful to those who have made the time to record for us how they have met some of them. Using their experience as a baseline, we again emphasise that three essential elements in working with children and families infected or affected by HIV are knowledge, initiative and flexibility.

Appendix A

The following guidelines were prepared by Sarah Ryan for respondents to base their answers on.

INTERVIEW GUIDELINES FOR ADOPTIVE PARENTS

I   About you – background information

How did you become involved?

Why/how did you decide to care for a child who is HIV positive?

How long has Billy/Amy been with you?

Did you know of his/her HIV status before placement?

If Billy/Amy was already in placement when did you discover his/her status?

How did you learn of his/her status?

How much information about HIV/AIDS did you have before placement?

What was your initial reaction to the knowledge that Billy/Amy was HIV positive?

How did you deal with initial worries concerning Billy/Amy's HIV positive status?

What was the involvement of social services at pre-placement/early stages?

Which other agencies were involved at this time?

What information/training/support/advice was given to you either before placement began, or on discovery of Billy's/Amy's HIV status?

Have you fostered/adopted before?

Who else is in your family?

II In placement

a) Confidentiality

What is your opinion on confidentiality? (Reasons for and against)

What were you advised to do/say by social workers/doctors etc?

Who have you needed/chosen to tell?

Why, and under what circumstances, have you disclosed information?

Did you discuss the decision with anyone else first (eg, neighbours with children, nurseries, family, babysitters, friends)?

Have you told them and what have you decided to tell them?

How did it affect you?

What were the reactions of the people you told?

b) Support and access to medical advice

How do you protect your child and yourselves (and others)?

What medical problems has Billy/Amy had?

What support do you receive from local general practitioner/ specialist consultant, health visitor, etc?

How often does Billy/Amy need treatment?

What relationship do you have with the medical staff?

How accessible is information to you?

What social work support do you have (or had before adoption)?

Is financial support available? (Where from?)

What counselling have you had at times of anxiety?

What advice have you had when making difficult decisions, eg, about who should know, starting school?

Whose responsibility is it to make these decisions?

Who do you turn to for support when in difficulty?

What support do you receive from friends, family?

Is there a support group with other carers?

What is the reaction/support in your local community?

Do you have access to a childminder, respite care?

What support would you like that you feel you don't have?

c) Feelings

What are your feelings about the future for Billy/Amy?

How do you approach the uncertainty about the future?

What is your attitude to others' misunderstandings about HIV infection and AIDS?

How do you feel towards his/her birth parents?

How/what have you told Billy/Amy about his/her illness?

What do you think you will tell Billy/Amy about his/her illness in the future?

How does Billy/Amy deal with his/her difficulties?

Does he/she – go to school?
         – play out with friends?
         – feel different?

What counselling have you had at times of anxiety?

What advice have you had when making difficult decisions eg, about who should know, starting school?

Appendix B

Bibliography

The following list is by no means comprehensive but contains a selection of useful titles.

Books for children and young people

Come sit by me by Margaret Merrifield, The Women's Press, 1990.
A story about a boy with AIDS. For children aged four to eight.

AIDS by Peter Sanders & Clare Farquhar, Franklin Watts, 1989.
For children aged seven plus.

The impact of AIDS by Ewan Armstrong, Franklin Watts, 1990.
Deals with the social effects of the virus and its global perspective. For children aged nine to fourteen.

What can I do about AIDS?, The Terrence Higgins Trust/Barnardo's, 1991.
For secondary school children and young people.

Make it happy, make it safe by Jane Cousin-Mills, Penguin, 1988.
Contains advice for young people on safe sex and HIV.

Books for adults

We include here only books relating to children, except for the last entry. The Terrence Higgins Trust has a comprehensive reading list on all aspects of HIV/AIDS. The list is available to enquirers, but the Trust does not supply the books.

HIV, AIDS and children: a cause for concern by Naomi Honigsbaum, National Children's Bureau, 1991.
A review of available services for affected children. Makes recommendations regarding necessary services.

Caring for children with HIV and AIDS, edited by Rosie Claxton and Tony Harrison, Edward Arnold, 1991.

A comprehensive guide for carers written by an experienced nurse/AIDS counsellor and a paediatric nurse/tutor.

AIDS in the family, The Terrence Higgins Trust/Barnardo's, 1991.
Information for parents and carers.

AIDS and HIV: information for foster carers, National Foster Care Association, 1990
A pamphlet giving basic guidance for carers.

Multilingual AIDS by Mehboob Dada, Health Education Authority, 1992.
Free booklet which comprehensively evaluates and reviews all the information on HIV available to black and minority ethnic communities.

Family Resource

Memory Store, Barnardo's, 1992.
A practical way of bringing together important information for children who are losing contact with their parents.

Organisations providing information and support

Many of the organisations listed provide services throughout the UK, although most are London based. Others, such as Positively Women, are planning to establish centres in other parts of the country. Specialist AIDS workers in local health authorities or social services will have information about HIV/AIDS projects in the different localities throughout the UK.

Aberlour Child Care Trust
Pioneering work in residential provision for drug dependent women and their children which has led to provision for any family affected by HIV/AIDS.

Brenda House
9 Hay Road, Niddrie
Edinburgh
Telephone 031 669 6676

ACET (AIDS Care Education and Training)
Provides professionally based, practical home care to people ill at home with HIV/AIDS-related illnesses.

P O Box 1323
London W5 5TF
Telephone 081 840 7879

ACT (Association for Children with Life-limiting Conditions)
Recently established information service for anyone concerned with such children.

Royal Hospital for Sick Children
St Michael's Hill
Bristol BS2 8BJ
Telephone 0272 221556

AVERT (AIDS Education & Research Trust)
Publishes leaflets and training materials relevant to work with young people; also interested in work with pregnant women.

11 Denne Parade
Horsham,
West Sussex RH12 1JD
Telephone 0403 210202

BAAF (British Agencies for Adoption & Fostering) Medical Group
A group of doctors concerned with children in need, operating within an umbrella child care agency.

11 Southwark Street
London SE1 1RQ
Telephone 071 407 8800

Barnardo's Positive Options Planning Scheme
Helps affected families to plan for their children's present and future. Also seconds experienced child care workers to other agencies working with HIV/AIDS. Publishes leaflets for children and families (see below).

354 Goswell Road
London EC1V 7LQ
Telephone 071 278 5039

Barnardo's St James Project
Support services for children, young people and parents affected by HIV/AIDS.

67 Bayswater Grove
Harehills
Leeds LS8 5LN
Telephone 0532 406777

BHAN (Black HIV/AIDS Network)
Black men and women provide information and support to black families affected by HIV/AIDS (see Helplines).

111 Devonport Road
London W12 8PB
Telephone 081 749 2828

Body Positive Women's Group
Supports women affected by HIV.

51b Philbeach Gardens
London SW5 9EB
Telephone 071 370 2051

British Pregnancy Advisory Service
Provides counselling regarding fertility issues and termination.

Austy Manor
Wootton Wawen, Solihull
West Midlands B95 6BX
Telephone 0564 793225

Brook Advisory Centres
Advice and counselling for young people on contraception.

153a East Street
London SE17 2SD
Telephone 071 703 9660

CAL (Catholic AIDS Link)
Catholic group offering non-judgmental, spiritual, emotional, practical and financial support to those affected by AIDS/HIV.

PO Box 646
London E9 6QP
Telephone 071 250 1394

Care AID
Support for those affected and infected
with HIV/AIDS. Can provide respite care.

12 Wrentham Avenue
Greenhill, Herne Bay
Kent CT6 7UU
Telephone 0227 375511

Carers National Association
Aims to develop appropriate support for
carers, including young carers.

29 Chilworth Mews
London W2 3RG
Telephone 071 724 7776

Compassionate Friends
Organisation of bereaved parents offering
friendship and support to parents
experiencing loss of a child of any age.

6 Denmark Street
Bristol BS1 5DQ
Telephone 0272 292778

Contact a Family
Provides links between groups of parents.

16 Strutton Ground
London SW1P 2HP
Telephone 071 222 2695

Council for Disabled Children
(Formerly Voluntary Council for
Handicapped Children) Consortium of
organisations concerned with disabilites
and medical conditions, including HIV/
AIDS. Provides information service.

8 Wakley Street
London EC1V 7EQ
Telephone 071 278 9441

CRUSAID
Leading fundraiser for AIDS causes.
Provides treatment centres, housing
schemes, education and research.

1 Walcott Street
London SW1P 2NG
Telephone 071 834 7566

The Globe Centre
A City and East London centre for people
affected by HIV/AIDS. Has support
groups and drop-in service.

148 Brick Lane
London E1 6RU
Telephone 071 377 2003

Grandma's
Voluntary organisation providing
practical help (babysitting, shopping,
transport, cooking etc) to families affected
by HIV/AIDS.

PO Box 1392
London SW6 4EJ
Telephone 071 731 0911

Haemophilia Society
Produces publications and provides
information for those affected by HIV/
AIDS through haemophilia.

123 Westminster Bridge
Road, London SE1 7HR
Telephone 071 928 2020

Health Education Authority
Organisation within NHS with responsibility for education on HIV/AIDS.
Publishes leaflets, training materials, etc,
also provides range of information.

Hamilton House,
Mableton Place,
London WC1
Telephone 071 383 3833

Jewish AIDS Trust
Provides counselling & education for the
Jewish community and financial support
for sufferers (see Helplines).

HIV Education Unit
Colindale Hospital
Colindale Avenue
London NW9 5HG
Telephone 081 200 0369

Lantern Trust
National organisation providing support,
education and training for carers.

72 Honey Lane
Waltham Abbey
Essex EN9 3BS
Telephone 0992 714900

The London Churches HIV/AIDS Unit
Ecumenical forum for support, advice and
further referral.

St Paul's Church
Lorrimore Square
Walworth,
London SE17 3QU
Telephone 071 793 0338

London Lighthouse
Centre for people with HIV/AIDS,
including people working in the field.
Provides training for volunteers,
workshops and lectures. Also has a
residential unit offering alternative
therapy.

111–117 Lancaster Road
London W11 1QT
Telephone 071 792 1200

Mildmay Mission Hospital
Pioneers in work with children, parents
and families (mother & child AIDS unit
due to open in 1993).

Hackney Road
London E2 7NA
Telephone 071 739 2331

National AIDS Trust
Independent organisation promoting
community education about HIV/AIDS.
Initiates and supports preventive work
projects in the UK. Information resource
for voluntary organisations. Staff includes
a development officer for children and
young people.

Room 1432, Euston Tower
286 Euston Road
London NW1 3DN
Telephone 071 383 4246

National Children's Bureau
Co-ordinates agencies working with
children and families affected by HIV.
Published *HIV/AIDS and children: a
cause for concern* (see Bibliography) and
initiated The National Forum on AIDS
and Children.

8 Wakley Street
London EC1V 7QE
Telephone 071 278 9441

National Forum on AIDS and Children
Promotes the interests and welfare of
children and young people in relation to
HIV/AIDS issues. It brings together UK
based organisations of user groups,
professionals and statutory/voluntary
bodies.

8 Wakley Street
London EC1V 7QE
Telephone 071 278 9441

National Foster Care Association
Information for carers of other people's
children. Publishes a leaflet for carers on
HIV/AIDS (see Bibliography).

Leonard House
5–7 Marshalsea Rd
London SE1 1EP
Telephone 071 828 6266

The Naz Project
Provides information and advice on HIV/
AIDS for South Asian (Indian sub-
continent) and all Muslim communities.
Also provides welfare, legal and
counselling help to individuals.

Palingswick House
241 King Street
London W6 9LP
Telephone 081 563 0191

*PARC (Paediatrics AIDS Resources
Centre)*
Information on all aspects of HIV/AIDS
with regard to children.

25 Hatton Place
Edinburgh EH9 1VB
Telephone 031 668 4407

Positive Youth
Offers information, support and groups
to young people with HIV/AIDS. Is part
of Body Positive.

51b Philbeach Gardens
London SW5 9EB
Telephone 071 373 7547

Positive Partners & Positively Children
Offers support (and small grants) to
children and young people in families
affected by HIV/AIDS under the auspices
of Positive Partners.

The Annexe
12–14 Thornton St
London SW9 OBL
Telephone 071 738 7333
also 100 Shepherdess Walk
London N1
Telephone 071 250 1396

Positively Irish Action on AIDS
Supports Irish people and families
affected by HIV/AIDS.

St Margaret's House
21 Old Ford Road
London E2 9PL
Telephone 081 983 0192

Positively Women
Free confidential support service for
women with HIV infection, ARC or
AIDS. Increasingly involved with
children (see Helplines). Produces leaflets
on women and HIV/AIDS.

5 Sebastian Street
London EC1V OHE
Telephone 071 490 5515

SCAFA (Scottish Child and Family Alliance)
Association of agencies which, among other functions, co-ordinates the work of its members with families affected by HIV/AIDS.

Princes House
5 Shandwick Place
Edinburgh EH2 4RG
Telephone 031 228 8484

The Terrence Higgins Trust
Provides information on all aspects of HIV/AIDS and is developing services for children, young people and families (see Helplines).

52 Grays Inn Rd
London WC1X 8JU
Telephone 071 831 0330

Helplines

BHAN Helpline
Monday–Friday 9.30am–5.30pm

Telephone 081 742 9223

Blackliners Helpline
Monday–Friday 10.30am–6pm For black
and ethnic minority communities

Unit 46,
Eurolink Business Centre
49 Effra Road
London SW2 1BZ
Telephone 071 738 5274

Body Positive Helpline
Monday–Sunday 7–10pm
Also drop-in help 11am–5pm
(open till 9pm Monday and Friday)

51b Philbeach Gardens,
London SW5 9EB
Telephone 071 373 9124

Childline
24 hours: for all children and young
people in trouble

Telephone 0800 1111

Jewish AIDS Trust Helpline
7.30–10pm

Telephone 081 200 0369

National AIDS Helpline

PO Box 1577,
London NW1 3DW

General service: 24 hours
Arabic: Wednesday 6–10pm
Cantonese/Mandarin: Tuesday 6–10pm
Bengali/Gujerati/Hindi/Punjabi/Urdu:
Wednesday 6–10pm
Hearing difficulties, minicom: daily
10am–10pm

Telephone 0800 567 123
0800 282 447
0800 282 446

0800 282 445

0800 521 361

Positively Women Helpline
Monday–Friday 12 noon–2pm

Telephone 071 490 2327

Terrence Higgins Trust Helpline
Daily 3–10pm

Telephone 071 242 1010

Legal help

Children's Legal Centre
Deals with social policy issues concerning
children.
Legal Helpline: weekdays 2–5pm

20 Compton Terrace,
London N1 2UN
Telephone 071 359 9392
Telephone 071 359 6251/2

Immunity
Legal advice centre for people affected
by HIV, including representation.
By appointment only, but can arrange
consultation at home/hospital.

260a Kilburn Lane,
London W10 4BA
Telephone 081 968 8909

Terrence Higgins Trust Legal Helpline
Wednesday 7–10pm

Telephone 071 405 2381

**DEPARTMENT OF APPLIED
SOCIAL STUDIES AND
SOCIAL RESEARCH
BARNETT HOUSE
WELLINGTON SQUARE
OXFORD OX1 2ER**